Perez

Crucial Conversations

Life Momentum

How to Get Going and Keep Going

by
David and Kenneth Smazik

authorHOUSE™

1663 LIBERTY DRIVE, SUITE 200
BLOOMINGTON, INDIANA 47403
(800) 839-8640
WWW.AUTHORHOUSE.COM

First published by AuthorHouse 11/15/05

ISBN: 1-4208-7615-5 (e)
ISBN: 1-4208-7616-3 (sc)

Library of Congress Control Number: 2005907072

Printed in the United States of America
Bloomington, Indiana

This book is printed on acid-free paper.

ACKNOWLEDGEMENTS

We would like to thank the following individuals for their kind assistance during this project. Ron and Connie Koehn, for initial encouragement and review of the first outline. Deanna Brady, for her expertise in the editing process. Gary Batty and Dr. Craig Herr, for review of early drafts. Jim Smith, for the generous amount of time he gave to a detailed overview of a later draft.

We also would like to express appreciation to our colleagues and parishioners over the years who helped shape ideas and lives. We especially give our love to Ann for sharing her skills and patience with us to finalize our thoughts.

TABLE OF CONTENTS

INTRODUCTION

"This time will be different."
"Now I know what I must do."
"I will begin tomorrow."
"If only I had _____, my life would be on track."

Do any of these statements sound familiar? If they do, then these are most likely also familiar:

"This time things were the same, after all."
"I guess I don't know what to do—nothing seems to work."
"Tomorrow, really...I'll start tomorrow."
"I need just one more thing, but I don't know how to get it."

The unsettling part of these statements is that they can be heard in attempts to clean up paperwork around the kitchen, or while attempting to gain control of the garage. Forgotten are the hopes and dreams of making significant changes. Can we gain traction for our aspirations, or are we doomed and forever buried by the "stuff" of life? Good intentions routinely stall, and familiar disappointment follows. A course of action stops short of completion. Have you noticed with each passing week that the sense of personal accomplishment dulls, and the clutter of life gains a little more ground?

"I was going to do that, but what difference does it make anyway?"

"When I get myself organized…like that will ever happen!"

Our past failures can cause us to question the well-known call to action, "Where there is a *will*, there is a *way!*" The *will* is there, but the *way* is elusive. *Paralysis of purpose*— the inability to achieve the things we deeply desire—often constricts our good intentions. Like in nightmares where one is unable to regain balance, most of us live our lives unable to gain movement toward a life of impact.

This book is about hope. There is hope for realizing your God-given potential. We will uncover that the same world that *appears* to conspire against you also offers you the opportunity to move out from under the piles and to keep moving forward.

What is your ultimate destination in life? Where do you want your life to go? How do you want to make a difference? How can you regain and build momentum to realize your conviction-driven goals? **Help for your journey is not only on the way—it is already here.**

More than ever, people struggle to uncover some positive way for their lives to progress well, but a current paralysis of purpose wins the day. When we become infected with this debilitating state of paralysis, our available energy seems to be sufficient only for the essentials. Did you once dream of organizing a program for your office, community, or place of worship? Now the mere thought of entertaining a few people in your home is a bit overwhelming.

A new hierarchy of basic needs has emerged in our contemporary culture: provide income for perceived necessities, give minimal effort to relationships, pursue hobbies or other means of distraction, and have little enthusiasm for much else. The satisfaction of accomplishing goals with impact—expressed in vocation, significant relationships, and community contribution—seems more and more elusive. Only a small minority pursue a higher, deeper calling; hope for more than the basics is in short supply for the majority.

A perspective that is neither original nor difficult to achieve can successfully attack the malaise that affects our hope for a life of impact. Like cures that are closer than first imagined, we already possess what we seek. The building blocks of a solution literally reside in our everyday field of vision—strands that when woven together portray a picture of hope amidst the confusion and commotion of contemporary life. There is a God-given dynamic in creation that enables us to *get going* and *keep going* to achieve impact.

More Than Meets the Eye

A few years ago, stereographic (hidden 3-D) pictures that seemed to consist of numerous random or repeated splotches were popular items in shopping-mall gift stores. They were first developed to study depth perception and published in *Magic Eye* books[1]. Some observers quickly detected the cleverly camouflaged three-dimensional images hidden in the seemingly flat patterns. Others strained and stared, but no images appeared—a paralysis of perception clouded their brains. Even the titles of the pictures that gave hints to the hidden forms sometimes failed to help viewers perceive the true subjects.

When observers finally relaxed, and their stress and preconceptions cleared, the optical illusions came slowly into view. A form that had always been present had been hidden behind a maze of perceptual static. Without the ability to relax and let a formerly imperceptible image appear to them, many would never distinguish the veiled forms within the flat sea of squiggles and colors.

Questions often lingered as people walked away from these fascinating tricks of the eye: "How did I miss something so obvious?" "How is it possible for that flat image to appear to be three-dimensional?"

Some stereographic artists gave various clues to observers to help them see the three-dimensional forms contained within the camouflaging bits of color and shapes on the flat surfaces of their pictures. To more easily perceive the subject of a stereogram, however, it's necessary to relax the focus of the eyes completely and look toward a point beyond the flat surface, into the distance (or "depths") to see the whole picture.

Contemporary living adds ever more splotches, in the form of an avalanche of information, to what already appears to be a complex and complicated picture of life. The image we seek, the vision of a multidimensional life of impact, is even harder to perceive. In the midst of so much static, how do we create lives with even a minimal amount of effectiveness?

Uncovering Momentum

Remember the need to relax the focus of your eyes. It is our hope that the familiar concept of *momentum* will begin to come into view. Picture a released object rolling along in a straight line with consistent direction and speed until some form of resistance builds up and interferes. This concept is not so mystical. Most individuals can identify with this reality from personal experiences, such as riding in a car or watching a sporting event in which it appears that one of the teams can do nothing wrong and cannot be stopped. Progress toward a desired goal moves at a consistent speed until resistance is encountered. The universal law of *inertia* produces this momentum of motion. You will need to peer a bit deeper into the mosaic of life to discover this very basic fact of our human existence. You might think, "How did I miss something so obvious?" We will have accomplished our purpose for writing this book if you begin repeating this phrase often.

Personal Inertia

Inertia operates most apparently in the physical realm. The more popular aspect of its definition is this one: *Objects at rest tend to remain at rest.* The lesser-known part of the definition, however, is the one that covers motion: *In the absence of an external force, objects in motion will maintain their speed and direction and travel in a straight line (take the most efficient path).* When an airliner touches down and the brakes and reverse-thrust engines kick in, you will typically lunge forward; your body wants to maintain its original speed and direction. When you make a split-second decision to exit the interstate, you might turn your vehicle off the highway, but your body wants to maintain its former direction. What happens to the person (or object) in the seat next to you if a seatbelt isn't in use? This three-dimensional picture often remains hidden in the busy murals of our lives.

Even when using common expressions related to inertia, like *"We're on a roll!"*, we easily fail to recognize that inertia operates throughout our lives. When resistance and friction are identified and removed, and we can claim and release our personal convictions of substance into action, those convictions will maintain their speed, direction, and straight-line efficiency. The result is a life of momentum—a life proceeding and arriving at its goals with impact. We can overcome the paralysis that keeps well-intentioned people motionless, unable to move beyond the basics of life.

Mentioned earlier, this kind of discovery brings a new perspective to already-present knowledge. Just as with the flat stereogram that suddenly reveals a multidimensional image, you might think to yourself, "It's incredible that the bigger picture has been hiding in there all along. How did I miss something so obvious?"

The Key—Use What You Already Know

The Webster New World Dictionary defines *momentum* as "the impetus of a moving object." This book explores in great detail the three dynamics of *life momentum*, or what could be described as the use of *personal inertia* in its broadest definition. Each chapter continues the expansion of this new way to conceptualize our lives, offering connections with everyday speech and action. Familiar phrases will open each chapter to continually remind us of how close we are to discovering this reality. We will also reveal known concepts and systems for you to apply in sections labeled "For Your Consideration." Questions at the end of each chapter will help integrate this perspective into the context of your individual experiences.

Return to the opening statements of this book. Consider these phrases from an emerging perspective of personal inertia:

"This time will be different." It's possible, but only after identifying our beliefs and values and how our level of passion actuates them. Amidst all the confusion of a fragmented, multiple-option world, what solid convictions make up the will of your life? This is the first dynamic, explored in Part One.

"Now I know what I must do." What you must do is relative to what you know deep within yourself. Align your will, or convictions, with this aspect of the first law of motion: *A body in motion tends to travel in a straight line and maintain direction and speed.* Assistance from this law awaits you after you place your passionate convictions into motion. Dynamic number two is explored in Part Two.

"I will begin tomorrow." You continue to move forward when you take time to identify what creates friction and what resists your movement toward a life of impact. Without knowing the forces that resist the action of your convictions, you cannot maintain momentum. Dynamic number three will be explored in Part Three.

"If only I had_____, my life would be different." The exquisite order of the universe is a gift to which we have access. Your willingness to return to the basics of motion to succeed in all aspects of life remains the key to the realization of your goals and dreams in a world ravaged by paralysis of purpose. The Creator God has provided much for us, including what we need to maintain motion through life, while impacting others.

The following chapters offer an opportunity to connect the dots that, previously, have made little sense—to discover what already exists: the *way* for the convictions of our *will*. Participate fully, as we combine many familiar items that have been languishing on the shelves of life. Discover existing concepts and systems that can assist us on our way.

A life of high impact awaits!

Questions

Introduction

1. Can you identify a program or project you once started or have always dreamed of doing?

2. When was the last time you plotted out the shortest route to a destination?

3. Recall an experience when you maintained your speed though you wanted to stop. (To prod your memory: skis, roller blades, skateboard, bicycle...)

4. How has an obstacle, some form of resistance, slowed your progress toward a goal?

PART ONE

Discover the Essentials to Get Going

CHAPTER ONE

Prepare for The Journey

"What am I made of?"
"Do I have what it takes?"

A formidable challenge stands directly in our path. Do we have what it takes to meet this challenge? Will the strength of our will maintain momentum until we reach our destination?

- Can you demonstrate mastery of a new skill or competency level in order to achieve that desired salary increase?
- Can you take the initiative to restore a broken relationship with a family member?
- Can you confront a community problem with involvement instead of countless hours of talk?
- Can you provide solid, personal responses to questions about purpose and ultimate meaning?

The phrase *paralysis of purpose* can describe our persistent inability to achieve the things we most desire. *How can you point your life in a new direction and begin to see movement?*

3

Consider what once gave guidance and direction to our lives:

Family—a deep sense of security and belonging, gleaned from knowing that the family unit would be supportive.

Community—the stability of living with an intergenerational mix of neighbors and relatives who had often occupied the homes around our towns for as long as anyone could remember.

Religion—born into a particular faith group with no thought of switching brands, or living entirely without a religious orientation.

Career—work for one employer for the majority of one's productive years, during which time personal identity and company affiliation become intertwined.

World Stability—for Americans, recognition that global conflicts are an inevitable part of life, but with the belief that such instability would not reach the shores of our country.

Today, we seek to develop direction in our lives even as our institutions and other underlying support systems fragment and dim. Compare this to another guiding light: lighthouses. These structures have become popular relics, great to include in a picture of the rising or setting sun. They remain, but often are not in use for navigational purposes. The once-invincible institutions of our society remain, but their power to provide clear direction has greatly diminished. The result: exhaustion, frustration, and eventual paralysis from efforts expended in vain to discover direction in the traditional manner. Like the structures and institutions that we seek to offer us purpose, the individual will can also become fragmented and disoriented. Our will may become simply a loose collection of ideas with no identified focus to create a life that has impact and momentum is lost. It is very difficult to conceive of a journey if your motivation is a bit foggy.

A Break in the Fog

A family camping trip on the shores of western Michigan is remembered for the foghorn that could be heard throughout the night. With the lighthouse rendered useless, this distinctive sound gave guidance. There are a growing number of voices that span the spectrum of life, alerting people to the need for a new orientation. Some segments of the business world now emphasize the personal development of the individual, not merely the socialization of the person into the culture of the company. In Reflections, The SoL Journal on Knowledge, Learning, and Change, Andre L. Delbecq states: "People need to understand what fundamentally resonates with them....I feel like I'm helping people perform self-exorcisms to get rid of the thing that tangles them up and pulls them down. I want them to be able to find their natural place."[2]

Jesus presents the core of Christian faith in two statements: "Love God with heart, mind, and soul," and "Love others as you love yourself." He does not simply put forth the institutional religion of his day, which consisted of countless laws. In church and business worlds, the contexts from which we write, we hear a call to discover a new orientation amidst an increasingly chaotic world. Even present-day pop psychology has arrived at this same place. Dr. Phil McGraw—a frequent guest on *Oprah,* who became the host of his own show—writes the following in his book *Self Matters*: "You can create a momentum that will allow you to be and do what you truly value and care about."[3]

To Get Going, Get Core Convictions

It is imperative that individuals develop and put into action well-defined and refined convictions that will continue in motion toward their destinations, irrespective of the multiple forms of resistance that currently threaten to impede personal effectiveness.

The will remains, albeit diminished and scattered, but this new day requires the will to be solidified into focused convictions. The *density* of your convictions determines your *destiny!* A nebulous or dependent will, lacking definition and substance, can be quickly stopped or diverted. *Do you have what it takes?*

For your life to gain momentum, solid convictions are necessary. You can't coast with direction that has been derived from traditional institutions. Your hope for a life of impact begins with clarity and solidification of your core convictions. To clarify this broad topic, we chose the following realms to explore: beliefs, values, and personal maturity.

Beliefs

Beliefs about self, others, the world, and that which is beyond human reason reside within us and motivate our actions. The power of our beliefs cannot be underestimated. Our beliefs serve as a guide for our lives. In the formation of convictions, three important tasks are necessary for this life inventory: weed out erroneous disbeliefs, identify the beliefs that remain, and clarify the beliefs that can serve as a focus for a life with impact.

To help organize your personal beliefs, consider a series of continuums. (A continuum places similar items on a sliding scale from one extreme to its opposite.) These continuums consist of the following:

- Beliefs about yourself: capable, intelligent, caring, inferior, unlovable.
- Beliefs about others: dependable, unique, stable, untrustworthy, self-centered.
- Beliefs about the world community: vast, different but not wrong, competent, hostile, apathetic.
- Beliefs about that which is beyond human reason:

real, present, centering, nonexistent, irrelevant.

While we begin to clarify beliefs, we must also take into account the false or erroneous beliefs that can exert influence in our lives. According to *The Lies We Believe* by Frank Minirth and Chris Thurman: "The primary challenge, then, is not to attempt changing the circumstances surrounding us, although there is nothing wrong with improving them when we can. The primary challenge is to make our mental tapes as truthful as we can so that we will be able to handle successfully whatever circumstances come our way."[4]

We believe that the rational branch of psychological therapy offers much to our current exploration. As you begin this work of identifying beliefs, be aware that many may actually be erroneous, such as the following: *"Finding a career with the right company will give me lifelong employment and personal identity."* What misbeliefs can you identify in your life? According to Ellis' Rational Emotive Behavior theory, the following is a list of commonly held, erroneous beliefs:

1. We must have love or approval from all people we find significant.
2. We must prove to be thoroughly competent, adequate, and achieving.
3. When people act obnoxious and unfair, we should blame and damn them, and see them as bad, wicked, or rotten.
4. We have to view things as catastrophic when we are seriously frustrated, treated unfairly, or rejected.
5. Emotional misery comes from external pressures, and we have little ability to control or change our feelings.
6. If something seems dangerous or fearsome, we must become preoccupied with it and make ourselves anxious about it.
7. It is easier to avoid facing life's difficulties and

responsibilities than to undertake more rewarding forms of self-discipline.

8. Our past remains all-important, and because something once strongly influenced our lives, it has to keep determining our feelings today.
9. People and things should turn out better than they do; we must view life as awful if we do not find good solutions to its realities.
10. We can achieve maximum human happiness by inertia (inactivity), inaction, or by passively or noncommittally "enjoying ourselves."[5]

Begin to focus on your beliefs. Remove those that are false, and clarify and further develop the ones that remain. Those beliefs have the possibility to become motivation for your life. They will form the core of your convictions. However, the inexact nature of this exercise can be frustrating until we determine whether our beliefs are valid. What validation exists for the accuracy of life directing beliefs a person may claim to hold?

Values

The answer is in our **Values**. Use of an abstract word such as values to validate beliefs might appear problematic at first; therefore, a concrete definition for "values" becomes necessary. We define values as those things or ideas on which we place importance, *confirmed by our daily actions.*

A major byproduct of our busy contemporary world is the high premium placed on time. This is a result of the effort required to weed through the endless assault of information and the lure of multiple options available to us and competing for our attention. The word *timesaving* almost guarantees a hearing or a look at any available product or service. Most organizations consider time-management abilities a prerequisite for employment. At the start of this new century, time has virtually replaced money as the most valuable commodity.

Now we have something concrete! Time has become the great equalizer; no person gets more or less of it. Each person has 1440 minutes a day, 10,080 minutes a week, and 524,160 minutes a year. How are these valuable minutes spent? Consider the familiar words of the writer of *Ecclesiastes 3:1–8* in the Old Testament.

> For everything there is a season,
> and a time for every matter under heaven:
> A time to be born, and a time to die;
> A time to plant, and a time to pluck up what is planted;
> A time to kill, and a time to heal;
> A time to break down, and a time to build up;
> A time to weep, and a time to laugh;
> A time to mourn, and a time to dance,
> A time to cast away stones, and a time to gather stones together;
> A time to embrace, and a time to refrain from embracing;
> A time to seek, and a time to lose;
> A time to keep, and a time to cast away;
> A time to rend, and a time to sew;
> A time to keep silence, and a time to speak;
> A time to love, and a time to hate;
> A time for war, and a time for peace.

Consider how you spend the time given to you. Notice how a short list of "values" that elucidates your beliefs emerges. Many individuals claim belief in the importance of personal competencies, but give no time to meeting new challenges or expanding their skills. Many place importance on family relationships, but commit few hours to activities with their families. Many claim to put their faith in God, but do not align themselves with a faith-based community and do not exhibit behaviors that signify a life commitment. People speak about world peace, but lack any form of involvement to make it a reality. Confusion and conflict exist between mere *interests* and the *values* based on beliefs.

Use the objective measure of minutes spent, and apply it to a list of the things and ideas you value. We mentioned that time has replaced money as our most valuable commodity. You can quickly discover what is truly important to you.

People might lay claim to an impressive list of beliefs, but the measure of invested time (what they are willing to act upon) might reveal fewer genuine, behavior-motivated beliefs. Value-based beliefs begin to uncover your *will*. For the *will* to find a *way* and maintain movement, it must be solidified into defined convictions.

Personal Maturity

The final realm to be considered in the clarification of our convictions is **personal maturity**. Personal maturity itself is a broad category. We propose that it consists of two sub-elements: emotional maturity and spiritual maturity. Like beliefs and values, maturity does not inherently come with clear assessment measures; yet we believe that consideration of spiritual and emotional development is necessary for a person to maintain effective direction in their lives.

Emotional Maturity

For your will to reach the critical level of density needed to be placed into motion toward impact, the mass of the interior life must contain a high level of emotional maturity. The lack of this maturity in contemporary society has reached epidemic proportions. From the counselor's office to business conference rooms, the ravages of this condition are legion. If people believe they are not the center of whatever universe they may be traveling in at a given moment, they often throw tantrums.

The roots of rampant immaturity run deep in America's recent history. Post-World War II prosperity and loss of communities (villages) with extended family to teach values all have contributed to the current overriding self-centeredness. In his book, *The Sibling Society,* John Bly describes how the recent generation of middle-aged adults recognizes nothing above or below themselves. They lack respect for those in positions of authority and lack compassion for those less fortunate.[6] The focus on accumulation of goods, even as the gap between the wealthy and poor widens at an alarming rate, is indicative of Bly's concern.

The plague of emotional immaturity has caught the attention of many. A major response and contribution to this growing concern comes from the work of Daniel Goleman, among others. His concept of emotional intelligence, founded on four competencies, gives a measure to the concept of emotional maturity. The characteristics of an emotionally intelligent person include the following:

- *Self-awareness:* attuned to inner signals; recognizes how feelings affect performance.
- *Self-management:* has emotional self-control; finds ways to manage disturbing emotions and impulses, and channels them in useful ways.
- *Social awareness:* has empathy that enables sensitivity to a wide range of emotional signals, allowing him/her to sense the felt, but often unspoken, emotions in another person or group.
- *Relationship management:* can inspire by creating interpersonal resonance and can move others with a compelling vision or shared mission. [7]

Spiritual Maturity

When there is an awareness of God's presence in the center of one's life, life management is turned over to God. This surrender will result in service to others. This is true social awareness and is most clearly evidenced through interpersonal relationships.

This book is based on the premise that we receive God-given potential through the created order of the universe. People tend to "come to life" when the focus moves outside themselves to others. But the darkness of self-absorption has overtaken this basic truth. The cloud of spiritual immaturity hangs low, choking off the created potential of many lives.

Life often reveals yet another perspective in the relationship that exists between spiritual and emotional development. The two-way flow between emotional maturing and spiritual maturing often becomes restricted; thus inhibiting the pervasive presence of God's grace. The result can be well-intentioned individuals with strong beliefs, accompanying values and a religious faith who devote little attention to emotional development. For the purpose of this book, the term *personal maturity* will subsequently represent a seamless union of spiritual and emotional development—the obvious presence within an individual of God's love and grace permeating one's interior life and its expression.

CONVICTIONS: Beliefs & Values & Personal Maturity

It is hoped that you have made an initial examination of your convictions. This process is lifelong and multifaceted. In our chaotic world, it has become more difficult to find a way for an undefined will. Placing your life in motion with the hope of impact requires solid convictions. Convictions do not stand as a separate facet of the interior life; convictions are the aggregate of beliefs, values, and personal maturity.

Remember the questions that began this chapter: "What am I made of? Do I have what it takes?" *Convictions are the stuff of which you are made, validated by your life. When you rid your life of unnecessary obstacles and friction, you can put your convictions into motion under the influence of the law of inertia and gain momentum toward your ultimate destination.*

In bringing our convictions to bear on our lives and the world, we want them to have the ability to maintain uniform motion (not to be slowed down or halted), and we want to attain our conviction-driven goals most efficiently (not get thrown off course). When we take action, we wish to maintain our momentum. Recall the property of inertia: a body in motion will remain in a straight line unless acted upon by some external force.

A critical adjustment we must make to bring definition to our convictions involves density and mass. To grasp and utilize the law of inertia in our lives, it is not a matter of possessing convictions but of possessing convictions that have great density.

In his book *A Brief History of Time,* well-known physicist Stephen Hawking illustrates the density of mass by describing the contents of a black hole in space:

> One such black hole could run ten large power stations, if only we could harness its power. This would be rather difficult, however: the black hole would have the mass of a mountain compressed into less than a million millionth of an inch, the size of the nucleus of an atom! If you had one of these black holes on the surface of the earth, there would be no way to stop it from falling through the floor to the center of the earth.[8]

The Impact of Solid Convictions

Consider a journey beyond the bounds of earth. Imagine stepping onto the space shuttle orbiting 175 miles above the surface of our planet; in this weightless environment, picture two balls of the same diameter. One ball is made of Styrofoam®(Registered trademark of the Dow Chemical Company.), while the other is a cannonball made of iron. Visualize a cannon on the space shuttle that will fire both. The balls are released with the same amount of acceleration, and they head directly at you. Do they arrive with the same amount of impact? No. Even in this weightless environment, the density of the iron cannon ball causes it to pack a greater wallop.

Our fictional example of a Styrofoam® and a metal ball illustrates the important concept of density. Styrofoam® consists mainly of voids or empty spaces, whereas a cannonball is made of iron. If we brought both of these balls to the Earth's surface, a scale would show the cannonball weighs much more. Iron is more dense than Styrofoam®. Both projectiles had the same initial velocity; however, the inertia is very different. The iron cannonball maintains greater inertia (ability to remain in uniform motion) than the Styrofoam® ball. More force is needed to slow or stop an object with more density.

The Needed Orientation Emerges

We have examined the beliefs, values, and personal maturity that merge together to create genuine convictions. Convictions define what a person is made of, and they must not be convictions in name only. To create momentum in life convictions of substance are essential, convictions that guide a life out of the grip of paralysis of purpose and convictions that contain mass and density and arrive at their targets with impact. Convictions solidify the will for action.

The laws of motion dictate that everything set in motion tends to move on a direct course unless it meets effective resistance and that everything stationary will remain in a state of inactivity unless propelled by a sufficient force. What do you attempt to put into action, a loose collection of lightweight convictions that resemble a Styrofoam® ball, or a cannonball of substantial convictions that arrives at its destination with impact, regardless of the context? Chapter Two will review in detail the type of effort necessary for the expression of these interior life convictions—our level of passion. Chapter Three will focus on the force of impact of our expressed convictions.

Before moving to these topics, take time to work through the following questions. We hope you will begin to discover convictions that contain the greatest potential density. Remember, the *density* of your convictions determines your *destiny*!

Questions

Chapter One

1. Which of these statement combinations best describes you?
    a. This time will be different. / This time, things were the same, after all.
    b. Now I know what I must do. / I guess I don't know what to do—nothing seems to work.
    c. Starting tomorrow, I will begin. / Tomorrow, really... I'll start tomorrow.
    d. If only I had _____, my life would be on track. / I need just one more thing, but I don't know how to get it.

2. If you were to undergo a life scan, where in your life would you detect *paralysis of purpose*?

3. Write an example of momentum/inertia that carried along an idea, life pursuit, or group of individuals to a place of impact.

4. Below are the three realms that constitute core convictions. Record your current status for each:
    a. Beliefs
        * Self:
        * Others:
        * World Community:
        * What Lies Beyond Pure Reason:
    b. Values (Catalogue hours)
        * Vocation:
        * Hobby/Interest:
        * Self-improvement:
        * Relationships:
        * Spiritual Life:

- Leisure:
c. Personal Maturity
    - Self-awareness   1 2 3 4 5 (highest)
    - Self-management   1 2 3 4 5
    - Social Awareness   1 2 3 4 5
    - Relationship Management 1 2 3 4 5

5. Considering the previous questions, what convictions begin to solidify?

6. Rate the strength (density) of your convictions: 1–5 (highest).

CHAPTER TWO

Build Your Speed

"I just can't get things going."
"That was a half-hearted attempt."

Convictions with substance are only half the challenge. The other half of the necessary motivation involves the presence of passion—the personal force required to put convictions into action. *"Let's get moving!"*

We need to develop movement for our convictions. In the physical universe, inertia is the tendency of an object's resistance to change in its current state of either rest or motion. The current state of your life is the issue. Unless there is interference, an object in motion will continue in motion, and an object at rest will remain at rest. *When applied force creates motion, there will be a natural tendency to maintain that motion, and momentum will build.* This chapter is about the force necessary to place a life in motion, and to establish momentum toward conviction-driven goals.

We can identify convictions derived from our beliefs, values, and personal maturity. However, just because we clarify our wills does not mean our lives start to move in a focused manner. As in the physical universe, without the presence of an accelerating force, we will have a natural tendency to allow our convictions to remain unexpressed. Consider the totality of the property of inertia. Inertia itself is neutral, but it can assist in supporting activity or inactivity.

The Needed Push

Remember that we are sharing a universal law. In a weightless environment, the obstruction of gravity's force is removed. Objects that lack any force to accelerate them will float without continuous motion in any one direction. For example, an astronaut in flight writes some observations with a pen. When she releases the pen from her grip, it remains floating at her side. Apply force to the pen—for example, launch it with a throwing motion—and it will continue in motion, maintaining its speed and direction in a straight line. A harmless writing implement now transforms into a mini-missile. In addition, the density of the released object will greatly determine the force of its impact when something intercepts it. This is why it is important not to merely have convictions, but to have convictions of substance.

To grasp the dynamic of acceleration, let's take a closer look at the subtle transition from a life frozen by paralysis to a life with momentum. The concept of acceleration takes on a new importance within the context of contemporary society. Malcolm Gladwell's book *The Tipping Points: How Little Things Can Make a Big Difference* describes the point at which a buildup of factors or the weight of an idea causes a shift from one perspective or direction to a new perspective or direction.[9]

Lost in our data dense contemporary life, we can easily find ourselves reaching a tipping point and getting caught in the current social epidemic of inaction—our emphasis shifting from putting our personal convictions into motion to a state of inactivity of the will. It is possible that our current ineffectiveness is a paralysis of purpose caused by the inability to process the overwhelming amount of information most of us are now expected to navigate.

Overloaded Systems

Consider further the extent to which this current paralysis is impacting the totality of human life. Why is it difficult to build momentum for our convictions? Below is a review of institutions that have lost some of their "push," exposing us to the current avalanche of information and data.

Corporations. Technology, the global marketplace, economic instability, and the information explosion have created a data-rich environment impossible to completely absorb. All that was formerly necessary for job security was a basic set of information. In the space of two generations, the information needed to stay current can virtually drown a person.

Family and relationships. A commitment to an endless vocational learning curve greatly affects family life. The time and energy required detracts from the establishment of solid relationship bonds. The task of maintaining the family for security and protection is much more complicated. This often results in relational groups continually breaking up and forming new family units. Blended families with multiple relational dynamics have become the norm.

Community. Society's mobility creates ever-new community configurations. Ties within family and beyond family become more difficult to establish and maintain. When downtime is available, the effort needed to process contemporary life often causes people to drop from exhaustion. The need to recharge overrides the need to form a network of interpersonal relationships. American society had switched from a front porch culture to a deck culture. The next turn in this evolutionary path has now taken place, switching from porch to deck to home-entertainment center.

Even during our downtime, the over stimulation continues with the endless number of Internet and television channel-surfing possibilities. Robert Putnam writes the following in *Bowling Alone*: "When the history of the twentieth century is written with greater perspective than we now enjoy, the impact of technology on communications and leisure will almost surely be a major theme."[10]

Religion. The Rockwellesque version of a town square complete with steeple church as the center of religious and social life is now difficult to find. A scan of the religious landscape adds another dimension to what was once thought of as a guide through life's storms. Religious affiliation through birth has now become increasingly rare. This automatic association was not always positive, but it did offer a sense of belonging to something enduring.

Traditional religious groups struggle with infighting and survival issues, and independent groups spring up continually. There are numerous denominational options, as well as the option of no affiliation. Often an eclectic collage of beliefs exists, with the fundamental tenets of openness and the premise that all type of behavior is acceptable if it doesn't appear to hurt another person. Religious organizations that can attract new members through entertainment, high excitement, and the expectation of low commitment have understandably become very popular.

Stuck on Open

Daily survival has become a challenge due to overabundance not scarcity. The tipping point has been reached. *The thought and effort necessary to commit to long-term purpose is in short supply.* A chain reaction is set off, and another tipping point reached. Inactivity becomes pervasive, experienced as stress or burnout that commonly manifests itself as a constriction or paralysis. Purpose has stalled in the data-dense, opportunity-rich milieu of contemporary society, and the break-up of our traditional institutions contributes to leave people adrift.

Over stimulation, created by today's information overload, swamps our ability to process and plan. This loss of momentum involves an aspect of inertia—objects at rest will remain at rest unless met by a compelling force. The challenge becomes twofold: filter life carefully in a high-stress era and counteract the aspect of inertia that perpetuates inactivity.

Unleash Your Passion

Personal passion is the force that sets in motion our focused convictions and lifts them from the information overload maze. Passion is the force that tips the shift from one aspect of inertia to the other. Passion is the force that breaks the hold of paralysis of purpose. Passion is the force that builds the momentum once supplied by institutions. Why use the word *passion*? In one respect, it refers to the idea of intense commitment to doing what you love.

Today, the usual connotation of passion refers to romance. Those who are consumed by passion, find it difficult to think of anything else, to envision anyone else but the one they love. They desire only to be in the beloved's presence; all else fades from interest. Passion motivates great sacrifice and the will to persevere against tremendous odds. Passion causes people to block out all distractions, to develop tunnel vision.

Professing our convictions can create resistance, both in ourselves and in others; therefore a willingness to sacrifice on behalf of our intense convictions becomes necessary if we are to act on them. We must develop the perseverance to power through the stimulation-loaded environment that has bogged down countless others, as well as overcome the aspect of inertia that keeps stationary objects in a state of rest. The depth of penetrating vision that comes with passionate convictions has special purpose-enhancing capabilities. It enables us to see our way through the fog that clouds the traditional points of orientation.

Proof of Passion

Incredible stories recount the passion—the singular focus and sacrifice against tremendous odds—of those who walk again after experiencing physical paralysis. Every fiber of their being focuses on the conviction that they will indeed walk once again. Countless hours of painful therapy consumes day after day, as this clear purpose consumes their lives. This is the type of passionate devotion necessary to achieve a life of purpose in our present environment.

A diversity of courageous people, once immobilized, can possess the perseverance to focus on a greater purpose amidst all the distractions. These individuals do not place blinders over their eyes. They are not oblivious to what confronts them. Rather, they have developed a depth of vision, a singular focus. Legions of us hunger to "walk again"—to become individuals with renewed passion, willing to sacrifice in order to act on our convictions effectively.

One truth remains the same in every age: convictions put into action by the force of passion will place us on the road traveled less frequently. Passion is the force that can allow a paralyzed person to walk again. Consider well-known individuals who have traversed the road less traveled, those who remained steadfast on their journeys. Their names represent passions that gave incredible force to their identified convictions. Many of these conviction-driven goals possessed a momentum that even death cannot bring to an end.

The passion of Sir Winston Churchill during World War II is evidenced in a phrase he delivered as part of a rallying cry for Great Britain in the face of incredible odds: "I have nothing to offer but blood, toil, tears, and sweat."[11] Emotional commitment, perseverance, and sacrifice—the components of passion—were the watchwords for a nation that withstood the Nazi onslaught. Churchill told his countrymen, "You ask, what is our aim? I can answer in one word. It is victory. Victory at all costs—victory in spite of all terrors—victory, however long and hard the road may be, for without victory there is no survival."[12] The Battle of Britain stands as an example of the power of passionate convictions to change the course of history.

Similarly, Martin Luther King confronted the deep hatred of prejudice, persevering with unabated passion. Marian Wright Edelman, in *Profiles in Courage for Our Time*, quotes Dr. King as saying:

> Human progress is neither automatic nor inevitable. Even a superficial look at history reveals that no social advance rolls in on the wheels of inevitability. Every step towards the goal of justice requires sacrifice, suffering, and the tireless exertions and passionate concern of dedicated individuals.[13]

Martin Luther King identified the importance of the force passionate individuals create to bring about change. Without passionate concern and dedication, our convictions will not persevere in the face of resistance.

Debates persist as to which individuals deserve canonization as saints. One twentieth-century candidate, who received resounding support even from outside the Roman Catholic Church, was Mother Teresa of Calcutta. Mother Teresa had a passion for the poorest of the world's poor. She strove to offer whatever help could relieve their suffering, often just to be present and simply hold the hands of those who were dying. The order started by Mother Teresa embraces poverty, so that no material possessions distract from the passion to serve. Mother Teresa wrote:

> Our progress in holiness depends on God and on ourselves—on God's grace and on our will to be holy. We must have a real living determination to reach holiness. 'I will be a saint' means I will despoil myself of that which is not God, I will strip my heart of all created things, I will live in poverty and detachment, I will renounce my will, my inclination, my whims and fancies, and make myself a willing slave to the will of God.[14]

Her singleness of purpose also led her to write, "Here in America...it is easy to let yourself get smothered by material things. Once you have them, you have to devote time to take care of them. And then you have no time for one another or for the poor."[15]

Jesus' disciple James wrote a letter to the early Christian church addressing the particular concern of those who claimed a belief, faith, but did not give evidence of their faith through passionate actions:

> What does it profit, my brethren, if a man says he has faith but has not works? Can his faith save him? If a brother or sister is ill-clad and in lack of daily food, and one of you says to them, "Go

in peace, be warmed and filled," without giving them the things needed for the body, what does it profit? So faith by itself, if it has no works, is dead. (James 2:14-17 RSV)

Throughout history there are individuals who have clearly exemplified passionate convictions in the face of obstacles that appeared insurmountable. The presence of their passion was the force that created these examples of life-changing momentum.

Present-day Passion

The road of passion in practice is also traveled by people we all know, but who do not come to the public's attention. A look below the surface in every community will reveal people who apply passion to their convictions to achieve their goals. They know the sacrifice, hard work, and emotional involvement required. They might be found on local school boards, working at food pantries, serving as tutors and mentors, fighting for literacy, or creating recreational opportunities; yet their ranks are thinning, as paralysis of purpose tightens its grip on communities.

The business world contains stories of those with passion who have persevered in atmospheres of downsizing, proliferation of world markets, and lightning-quick change. In their book *Good to Great*, Jim Collins and Associates recount the passion of Darwin Smith to save a paper company by making business decisions considered ludicrous by industry insiders:

Smith brought that same ferocious resolve to rebuilding Kimberly-Clark, especially when he made the most dramatic decision in the company's history: Sell the mills. Shortly after he became CEO, Smith and his team had concluded that the traditional core business--coated paper--was doomed to mediocrity. Its economics were bad and the competition weak. But, they reasoned, if Kimberly-Clark thrust itself into the fire of the *consumer* paper-product industry, world-class competition like Procter & Gamble would force it to achieve greatness or perish.

So, like the general who burned the boats upon landing, leaving only one option (succeed or die), Smith announced the decision to sell the mills, in what one board member called the gutsiest move he'd ever seen a CEO make.[16]

In their book *Primal Leadership,* Goleman, Boyatzis, and McKee recount the following story of one CEO who was willing to do whatever it took to improve service:

Consider the example of Bob Pittman, then-CEO of Six Flags Entertainment. Hearing that the janitors at the amusement parks were being surly to customers, Pittman decided to get a ground's-eye view of the problem: He went undercover as a janitor. While sweeping the streets, he began to understand the problem.[17]

Accelerate Your Convictions

The personal profiles shared in this chapter emphasize the necessity of taking action based on our convictions, using a force defined as passion. Passion applied to convictions regains movement toward a purpose.

As established, the mere identification of convictions will not accomplish our long-term purpose. The force needed to push an object at a given acceleration rate is proportional to the object's mass. Convictions with substance will insure greater inertial potential.

A similar truth applies to the push necessary for placing our convictions in motion and keeping them in motion. The more force we apply, the more our inertial potential increases. Personal passion provides the high degree of force needed to move us out of our lethargy and accelerate us toward our goals. The greater the passion, the greater the force behind our convictions. *An all-consuming passion will apply the optimal thrust to our convictions of substance, which will result in maximum impact and achievement of purpose.* These are the elements necessary to create unstoppable momentum!

From Powerlessness to Passion

How can we make this kind of change a reality? How can paralysis be made to loosen its grip and discontinue inhibiting the potential of our lives? What exists that can break the current habits of inactivity for the things that matter in life? The thought of a new life direction energized by a renewed passion might not seem possible. Consider two tried and true methods that can assist in reorienting one's life pursuits.

Systems of behavioral change that have histories of proven success include the twelve steps of Alcoholics Anonymous. A strong spiritual component dominates the program. This system has been expanded and used to assist individuals in changing a variety of behaviors. (The words *alcohol* in Step One and *alcoholics* in Step Twelve can simply be changed to other words that represent a different type of addiction, compulsion, or negative behavior). One of its basic assumptions is that a dependency or addiction exists, which creates a strong gravitational pull. In all variations of these steps, change (developing acceleration) begins with an admission of powerlessness against dependency.

David and Kenneth Smazik

[For Your Consideration]

The twelve steps for recovery are:

1. We admitted we were powerless over alcohol—that our lives had become unmanageable.

2. We came to believe that a Power greater than ourselves could restore us to sanity.

3. We made a decision to turn our will and our lives over to the care of God as we understood Him.

4. We made a searching and fearless moral inventory of ourselves.

5. We admitted to God, to ourselves, and to another human being the exact nature of our wrongs.

6. We were entirely ready to have God remove all these defects of character.

7. We humbly asked Him to remove our shortcomings.

8. We made a list of all persons we had harmed and became willing to make amends to them all.

9. We made direct amends to such people wherever possible, except when to do so would injure them or others.

10. We continued to take personal inventory and when we were wrong promptly admitted it.

11. We sought through prayer and meditation to improve our conscious contact with God as we understood Him, praying only for knowledge of His will for us and power to carry that out.

12. Having had a spiritual awakening as the result of these steps, we tried to carry this message to other alcoholics and to practice these principles in all our affairs.[18]

In our case, as in AA, we first need to admit our current situations to ourselves. What do we believe about ourselves and the world? What holds us down, keeps us from developing momentum? Recall your examination of your convictions. What erroneous beliefs that support unhealthy, unproductive behaviors, render you motionless?

To beat paralysis of purpose, a sponsor or mentor might become a critical component in our lives. The brief personal profiles shared earlier in this chapter illustrate the power of those who lived lives of impact. Identifying and aligning ourselves with individuals who live their convictions with passion can provide us with helpful clues to establishing greater effectiveness and movement toward a life of impact. The use of life coaches and life strategists is becoming more common as people recognize their need for help in recovering their purpose and learn how to take effective action toward their goals.

The second example of an effective method for change is contained in the more recent book, *Changing for Good*. When this system is compared with the traditional steps of the AA program, many similarities become apparent. (See end of chapter.)

To shift from inactivity to activity and release your convictions into action, it all comes down to your level of passion. To break the pull that holds you down and holds you back, and to turn the wheels of purpose within and outside of your life, your individual convictions need to accelerate through sacrifice, suffering, and selfless exertion.

David and Kenneth Smazik

The norm in contemporary life has become powerlessness over all that now swirls around us. When our convictions seek expression, the weight of the Information Age calls for nothing less than total commitment. It's time to define convictions and live life with our *whole hearts*!

[For Your Consideration - The Six Stages of Change]

Precontemplation	People at this stage usually have no intention to change their behavior and typically deny having a problem.
Contemplation	In the contemplation stage, people acknowledge that they have a problem and begin to think seriously about it. Contemplators struggle to understand the problem, to see its causes, and to wonder about possible solutions. Many contemplators have indefinite plans to take action within the next six months or so.
Preparation	Most people in the preparation stage are planning to take action within the very next month and are making the final adjustments before they begin to change their behavior.
Action	The action stage is the one in which people most overtly modify their behavior and their surroundings. In short, they make the move for which they have been preparing.
Maintenance	It is during maintenance that people must work to consolidate the gains they attained during the action stage and other stages, and struggle to prevent lapses and relapses.
Termination	The termination stage is the ultimate goal. Here, the former addiction or problem will no longer present any temptation or threat; the behavior will never return, and people will have complete confidence that they can cope without fear of relapse.[19]

Questions

Chapter Two

1. Describe a "half-hearted attempt" from your own life experience.

2. How have the following areas of life become more challenging to navigate?
   - Corporations:
   - Family/Relationships:
   - Community:
   - Religion:

3. What has your "whole heart," the focus of your attention?

4. List individuals from history that clearly had focused passion.

5. Which of your convictions energizes you?

6. What might you need to admit to yourself to allow convictions to accelerate with passion?

CHAPTER THREE

Ready for Impact

"Without her, this never would have been accomplished."
"He's like a pit bull who doesn't let go until the task is completed."

A Personal Perspective

Individuals with the tenacity to achieve consistent, high-quality results will always stand out against the backdrop of current cultural confusion. Those able to live a balanced life with high impact are a rare commodity. In light of most of our efforts to simply navigate contemporary life, we might assume that such extremely effective individuals must have been born with a rare gene. There seems to be no other explanation for someone who sustains a consistent level of impact fueled by passion.

What separates these people from the masses who struggle through the morass of daily life? Why do only a small minority live lives of such high impact, regardless of the context? What do a small percentage of individuals perceive on their life journeys that eludes the rest of the population?

These questions led us to seek answers. We consider ourselves curious observers who labor in diverse fields, yet discovered a commonality in the questions and concerns we share. In our case, a Fortune 500 company and a mainline Protestant denomination occupy seemingly opposite points on the vocational continuum. Issues such as profit margins, globalization, technological advances and downsizing versus Christian education, missions, worship styles, and sustainable growth for survival, have traditionally been diametrically opposed. While the organizational structures and missions of our employment differed dramatically, on closer scrutiny undeniable similarities began to surface in the people of impact who sustained forward motion.

In the past two decades, the business world was progressively learning to recognize the need of individuals to develop personal values apart from the corporate vision. Stephen Covey's books *The Seven Habits of Highly Effective People* and *First Things First* exemplified this shift to "value-centered leadership."[20] Soon, religious organizations began looking to the business world for help in developing vision statements that would work in a quick-change world and for hints in downsizing or right-sizing organizational structures for increased effectiveness.

More and more cross-pollination has taken place, as all sectors of society have sought organizational orientation points to navigate in the new global paradigm. Religious organizations now use consultants to advise on future organizational initiatives, and the business world encourages employees to take time to develop personal character.

Even in our disparate pursuits, the authors found that we could make a common observation: across the vocational continuum, individuals appeared to experience a life paralysis that constricted the way for their will. Those who attempted to live lives of impact often lacked both solid convictions and the fortitude to maintain forward motion.

Paralysis of purpose appears to be spreading with no sign of relief in sight. Continuing education seems more important than ever, yet appears to be less effective than before. Employees who might have to assume additional responsibilities because of downsizing, and who already struggle to keep moving with the growing weight of the Information Age upon them, are finding it difficult to implement and sustain new techniques.

Consider another observation that straddles our vocational spectrum: *A small segment not only demonstrates momentum toward clear purpose, but also consistently arrives at a destination with high IMPACT.* While disorder reigns around them in the form of increased expectations, these individuals, manage to move in sync with nature's deeper law of momentum, which allows them to sustain personal progress while many others suffer from entropy of hope. This minority does not focus all their time on adding new techniques to their personal repertoires; rather, they seem to clear away the extraneous to allow their identified convictions to maintain mobility.

These people are not oblivious to external factors; rather, they incorporate only necessary and critical information into their well-defined, internal convictions. Circumstances might form and reform, yet these individuals demonstrate the acumen and ability to maintain purposeful motion to achieve a life of impact. The consistent result is high-impact success. *For them, all this appears to be quite simple and natural...because it is!*

David and Kenneth Smazik

The X-Factor

The force of impact increases in relationship to both the mass and density of an object (the weight of our identified convictions) and the acceleration at which the object is traveling (propulsion at the level of our personal passion to act on our convictions).

Now we simply need to do the math to arrive back at the questions we originally asked regarding those who possess life momentum. These individuals might not demonstrate mastery in a vast range of competencies or hitch future success to every new trend that comes down the road, but what they do believe in and value translates into action with a velocity that demands attention and delivers results.

This group appears to discern what the law of inertia, available to all, allows them to accomplish. *Inertia has become their X-factor—a law of the universe virtually unknown in its application to daily effectiveness, but a constant, and one that influences the motion of purpose. This X-factor of inertia, the unknown variable added into life, produces the possibility of future impact.*

Consider these examples of our emerging X-factor from the physical world: Two vehicles hit the side of your home. One is a Mini-Cooper with a velocity measured at about five miles per hour. In this case the force of impact is minimal; there will probably be little effect on the house, although the little car will undoubtedly be damaged in the process. Low density combined with low velocity equates to low-impact force.

In the second instance, a fully loaded cement truck accelerated to fifty miles per hour slams into the wall of your house. The high density of the object combined with its high velocity equates to a high-impact force. The wall will most likely collapse, and possibly the entire home. Even if, at the last second before impact, the driver turned the wheels, the inertia operating on the mass of the vehicle would maintain its direction and speed, and it would continue on its path into your living space.

The Evidence Mounts

The weightless environment of space also confirms the X-factor and the truth of the life equation presented in this chapter. An astronaut may be in need of two particular objects: the pages from the flight plan for a particular day and a camera to capture some of the day's projects. An overzealous flight specialist spots the needed floating objects and then volleys both items in the direction of the astronaut. Which would you rather catch—a few pages of paper, or the camera?

Force of impact, the product of mass and velocity, is a reality that operates predictably in the known universe. It is the X-factor that some people appear to understand intuitively. In the process, they collapse the walls of resistance that stand in their way (like the cement truck), while others appear to bounce off the walls with little impact except for the potential damage to the weaker convictions (like the car).

Everyday Examples of Impact

The following illustrations represent four spheres of life referenced in Chapters One and Two.

Vocation. A corporate executive assumes management of a multinational group responsible for technical services. She values both the employees she manages and the buyers who utilize her corporation's services. She has a strong belief in her company's support of its vendors, especially international suppliers. Taking extra time for research outside her field, she discovers an innovation that uses available technology to disseminate needed updates in a simple fashion and a highly usable form. The innovation brings the corporation success well beyond previous levels and consequently shines a light on this individual's management style.

What allowed this high-impact result to replace the status quo of previous relationships? It was the manager's core convictions. Her belief was based on a value that required a commitment of extra time to investigate uses of technology that did not relate directly to her primary area of expertise. This belief and value system was framed by personal maturity; the manager knew that other departments would need to be involved, and the approach and execution required clear communication and careful handling of egos. For this manager, disseminating improved information to a worldwide network became a passion. The velocity of her actions increased through a personal commitment of time and through the enlistment of various individuals. The result: a conviction of substance propelled and accelerated by passion, arrived with sustainable high impact.

Family. A father fears that his teenage daughter has begun to write him out of her life. Just at a time when adult conversations can occur and life lessons could be shared, the communication channels begin to shut down. The father values his relationship with his daughter, so he establishes dedicated weekly time together, a compromise of interests that begins the rebuilding process.

This father believes that a parent must develop a solid personal relationship with a child to ensure mutual respect and self-esteem, not merely go through the motions of parenting. His conviction is evidenced by acting on beliefs and values, even if it means he will need to drop a hobby or cut down on hours at work, although this tradeoff might impact future job promotions. His beliefs and values are framed by personal maturity—his willingness to sacrifice other interests and his perception of his daughter's need to be treated more like an adult than a little girl. He spends time reading about parenting and improves his listening skills, which bring him a new understanding of his daughter and her interests. His convictions regarding the preservation and development of this important relationship have become a passion. The result: A conviction of substance, motivated and accelerated by passion, begins to have great impact.

Community. A former gang member personally knows the high cost of violence. His belief is that violence begets violence, and intervention is necessary to break this cycle. He highly values the lives of his community's children and families. The only hope he can see is early intervention and teaching conflict-resolution skills. Actuating his convictions, he begins designing programs that allow children to come together and learn nonviolent means to resolve differences. He gathers support from a wide variety of organizations: government, religious, business, and secular nonprofit groups.

This project becomes his passion. He begins a program in which at-risk children can learn to resolve conflicts through peaceful means. Seeking a location, initiating trial programs, and developing a broad base of support requires all the personal maturity he can muster. He must function in environments in which he has no experience of his own. Finances are tight and verbal commitments often lack follow-through, but the first signs of positive results fuels his passion and propels his actions toward the goal. The result: a ministry poised not only to impact one city but to spread to others.

Religion. A mother frets over the media role models that parade in a constant stream before her children. She overhears snippets of their conversations with friends she formerly considered well behaved, deepening her concerns. Her children seem to lack a deep moral foundation, and the ill winds blowing around them continue to increase in intensity.

She values her children's lives and their future happiness above all. She believes that their survival and success depend on moral development, reinforced with a connection to a deeper reality beyond the role models of contemporary society. She seeks out a church in which to involve her family.

This woman's beliefs and values are framed by a maturity that allows other authority figures to be involved in the raising of her children. Her convictions are evidenced by the time she commits to a weekly schedule that accommodates participation in a church, and the effort she has made to seek out a comfortable spiritual fit for her family. Her passion about her children's welfare is energized each time the TV is on and by accounts of kids from supposedly stable families who lacked the moral rudder to make good choices. The first papers her children bring home from church classes apply religious truths to everyday experiences, and a new foundation begins to take shape. The result: Her convictions, fueled by her passion, had an impact in the lives of her children who in turn began to help others through service opportunities.

A Common Theme

Each of these examples demonstrates, not only the impact of convictions motivated and accelerated by our passion, but also the maintenance of motion and the removal of resistance through personal maturity and commitment. These situations were not resolved by extreme, one-time actions. Rather, they exhibited maintenance of motion, the X-factor.

The necessities of basic survival in contemporary society do not easily allow individuals to step back from the daily grind and examine life from a new perspective. The ever-present challenges of daily life tend to cloud our vision and obscure the orientation points on which we once relied. Recall the stereographic pictures we mentioned in this book's introduction. What appears at first as a nondescript collection of splotches can reveal a multidimensional picture if we are able to relax our vision, change our perspective, and look "into the distance," beyond the surface to the true image. Similarly, in contemporary society, to quote a well-known phrase, we often have trouble seeing the forest for the trees. Many of us struggle to regain our bearings, not knowing where to look as we strain to see clearly.

High-Impact Leaders

Jim Collins and Associates wondered what precipitated the movement of a company's success from solid to spectacular. In their book, *Good to Great*, they constructed a study consisting of various criteria for a judgment of *good* and one of *great*. They conducted an investigation in which control-group companies were also utilized, and companies' excellence levels were calibrated with concrete measurements that included profits.

How did companies step up to greatness? One interesting factor involved the CEOs of the companies that made this move. Not surprisingly, CEOs of the great companies exhibited what we refer to as *convictions of substance* and *personal passion*. They were not flamboyant, charismatic individuals who lived on the edge. "Level 5 leaders set up their successors for even greater success in the next generation, whereas egocentric Level 4 leaders often set up their successors for failure."[21] The CEOs of the great companies were people who maintained motion toward a goal that would continue beyond their own tenure.

Below are key points that Collins and Associates discovered in leaders of great companies, (labeled as Level Five leaders), and what we describe as high-impact leadership.

[For Your Consideration]

- Level Five leaders embody an almost paradoxical

43

mix of personal humility and professional will. They were ambitious, to be sure, but their ambitions were first and foremost for the company, not for themselves.

- Every good-to-great company had Level Five leadership during its pivotal transition years.
- Level Five leaders set up their successors for even greater success in the next generation, whereas egocentric Level Four leaders often set up their successors for failure.
- Level Five leaders displayed an inspiring modesty and were self-effacing and understated. In contrast, two thirds of the comparison companies had leaders with inflated personal egos that contributed to the demise or continued mediocrity of their companies.
- Level Five leaders were almost fanatically driven to succeed, imbued with a relentless need to produce sustained results. They resolved to do whatever it took to make the company great, no matter how great or difficult the required decisions.
- Level Five leaders display[ed] a workmanlike diligence—they were more plow horse than show horse.[22]

Taking on Giants

A perfect example of high impact leadership can be found in the biblical account of a shepherd boy, David, as he faced the giant, Goliath. Goliath was a formidable foe. An entire army was paralyzed with fear at the sight of the huge man-beast. A fearsome enemy unmatched in combat skill, he faced them complete with weapon and armor.

One person saw the situation from a very different perspective than the others. David considered the size of the huge man and determined that his forehead was a large exposed target for a hurled stone. Goliath was also very slow compared to the fleet-footed animals David was accustomed to hitting with rocks while protecting his sheep. In that sense, this was no contest. With fearful brothers and a trembling army behind him, David faced Goliath and brought down the giant that stood in the way of the army of Israel.

During his lifetime, many other "giants" would stand before David: a king who was obsessed with his destruction, struggles for power within his own family, and a battle with lust that cost him dearly. Yet David continued to observe life from a different perspective, a view that allowed motion toward the object of his passion: the development of a nation that would achieve an unparalleled size and power, which had previously been only a dream.

David was called from among his nation to be a leader. His belief occupied the center of his world. He possessed convictions of substance. His passion was sometimes misplaced, but he would do whatever was necessary to establish his people as a powerful force. David faced giants, yet maintained motion toward the purpose he believed he was called to fulfill. The result: the impact of this life was a powerful nation that never again reclaimed such a position of dominance after the reign of this boy who became king.

In the Presence of Giants

While most of us believe ourselves overmatched in the presence of "giants," there are those who live lives of impact despite daunting opposition. They stand out from a crowd paralyzed with fear. This rather small group appears to operate from a perspective even they may only partially understand.

The contemporary world is replete with huge and daunting challenges. To move apart from the paralyzed crowd will require nothing less from us than firm convictions and sustained passion to put them into action. The result can be a force of impact in the foreseeable future that is unparalleled in our personal history.

Part One and Beyond

Part One of this book moves you apart from the crowd to initiate introspection and identify and accelerate the convictions that will allow you to confront challenges standing in your path. Part Two lays out a strategy for maintaining your direction and speed even as giants threaten to impede your progress. Part Three explores the types of resistance that need identification and removal in order to continue your momentum toward the fulfillment of your conviction-driven goals. It also presents a further comprehensive view of what people of impact may not fully grasp even while they embody it: the X-factor, inertia, and the constant reality of the universe that influences our motion toward realization of our purpose.

Questions

Chapter Four

1. Name a person in your sphere of life that consistently arrives with high impact, unaffected by paralysis of purpose.

2. How was the reality of the X-factor, the often undetected presence of inertia (momentum), been manifested in your life?

3. What areas of your life would you like to take from good to great?

4. What "giants" in your life thwart your efforts to arrive with impact?

PART TWO

Discover What Keeps You Going

CHAPTER FOUR

Avoid the Debris

"Go with the flow."
"Get on track."
"Allow the momentum to carry you along."

Is our journey one that is energized with passion and pointed toward conviction-driven goals? How do we stay firmly centered on this road while avoiding the debris in our path and a host of detours?

Maintenance of Direction and Speed

To explore the concept of inertia/momentum further, let's examine our experience with motion in the physical world. Vehicles, planes, bicycles, roller blades—anything that places us in motion highlights our awareness of an object's *tendency to maintain direction and speed*. Braking and turning remind us that bodies desire to maintain the speed at which they were traveling, as well as the direction in which they were heading.

In the metaphysical world, *motion* submits to the same unchanging dynamics. Ideas and the pursuit of meaning also have a tendency to maintain direction and speed. Once in motion, ideas and the pursuit of meaning are often difficult to stop or divert. A particular person with an idea or conviction may encounter a barrier or diversion, but an idea with substance continues to maintain momentum.

The *Way* for the *Will*

The laws of motion operate throughout life and do not discriminate. These realities exist whether we're driving an economy compact or super-charged sports model, and whether we're initiating a new personal exercise program or one to improve community housing. These laws exist when focused beliefs are embodied or when no beliefs in particular are identified. The pieces to this puzzle of achieving effectiveness with assistance of a universal law now appear on the table. The question remains: Do we know what we have, and can we construct the picture of effectiveness? Can we bring forth all the dimensions from the mosaic of life, the challenge presented in the introduction of this book? This opportunity remains constant even during a time of continual change; the *way* for the *will* is ours to access.

A Daily Occurrence

We experience this law of motion in countless ways on a daily basis. While we might not be aware of its presence, inertia is a natural part of our existence. Each time a person buckles up in a vehicle, there is a tacit recognition of the reality of inertia, and the potential force involved. At the time this chapter was being conceived, an unfortunate example of inertia made the national news. In Nebraska, a section of Interstate 80 collapsed in minutes after a ten-inch downpour of rain. A tractor-trailer loaded with potatoes was unable to stop before sliding into the cavern that suddenly appeared where, only moments earlier, a solid stretch of four-lane highway once existed. Even though the driver applied his brakes, the weight of the loaded rig had created a high level of inertial energy that maintained its original direction and speed. The result was disastrous.

While rarely acknowledged, except when the high speed of present-day travel comes to an abrupt halt, the reality of inertia in the physical world is accepted. In contrast, the relationship of this physical reality to the totality of life is neither acknowledged nor accepted.

Interrelationships

Consider the growing body of credible evidence of various relationships between natural realities in the physical world and human life. The phases of the moon during its orbit around Earth appear to affect more than tides. Schoolteachers and hospital emergency-room personnel can often identify when the moon is full or near the full phase. Human behavior seems clearly tied to the natural order of the orbit and rotation of Earth and the moon. And there are often many more accidents, injuries, and instances of misbehavior during a full-moon phase.

Another natural occurrence that appears to influence the behavioral patterns of individuals is Seasonal Affective Disorder: our sensitivity to the presence or lack of sunlight and its effect on mood. Locations and seasons of the year that result in lower levels of sunlight due to the rotation and orbit of Earth seem to intensify symptoms of depression. People who suffer from chronic depression seem especially susceptible to this syndrome. The longer periods of darkness around the winter solstice (also the holiday season) often prompt an increase in symptoms of depression. Even some who do not suffer from clinical depression can find themselves experiencing an extremely dark mood.

This overview brings us to the core of momentum for your life, the *total life* influence of the law of inertia that relates to maintenance of direction and speed. Consider ideas or convictions that consist of heavy, solid substance **or** lack weight and density. These convictions are released into the stream of human existence. Similar to the Styrofoam® ball, the one that lacks cohesion will quickly fade when encountering any form of resistance. When given the same amount of push, however, the idea or conviction with substance and weight has the possibility to move through resistance and maintain its direction and speed. These convictions retain their focus and arrive with impact.

The founders of the United States of America held convictions with enough substance to carry the country into its third century. One such conviction was, "government of the people, by the people, and for the people." Patriots, including Patrick Henry, expressed passion for these ideals with such phrases as, "Give me liberty, or give me death!" These convictions have endured threats from without and from within, and they continue to endure. At times, patriotism can wane, but the momentum of these convictions remains strong.

Examples abound within virtually every community. Quality healthcare, education, recreational facilities, religious opportunities, programs to assist the underprivileged—all have been championed by individuals with convictions of substance that continue to this day.

Throughout the history of humankind, personal inertia has also delivered the impact of destructive convictions. Slavery, racism, and male dominance have been some of the results. The amount of force necessary to deter and stop these ideas is evidence of the amount of inertial movement they achieved and continue to maintain. Nationalism (spurred by religious intolerance and racism) maintains its direction and speed even as new generations become victims of hatred and murder.

Individuals of passionate convictions, who consistently maintained their life momentum substantiate the effects of personal **impact** throughout history. The opposite is a loose conglomeration of interests released and accelerated with little passion or effect. We've all heard the phrase, "nothing but a lot of hot air." The result is substantiated through an even greater number of examples of individuals who lack purpose and who thus consistently exert low force, achieve low impact, and never start or become lost on their journeys.

An important fact to recall is that, similar to the rotation and orbit of Earth, inertia always exists and always exerts its influence. There are physical and metaphysical consequences of this truth. What is it that we consistently release under the influence of this law of motion? How have we utilized the dynamics of inertia, the X-factor—maintenance of direction, speed, and a straight line?

Four Emerging Realities

We remember sitting in many classrooms when a particular subject's presentation turned from crystal clear to murky. This change was often due to one of the following: exceptions to the rule or one more piece of information that must be remembered. The universal law of motion we have been describing should be obvious; yet the reality of personal inertia's potential is camouflaged, increasingly shrouded, largely because of four present-day realities. This list is not all-inclusive but represents a reasonable overview. The four realities, previously referenced, play ever-increasing roles in the onset of paralysis of purpose: fragmentation of institutions and structures; options and choices on a continual increase; data density in an environment of information overload; and an accelerating rate of change.

Personal inertia, however, has the potential to continue the momentum of purpose through these four emerging realities: fragmentation, multiple options, data density, and chaotic change. We can "take heart". We do not need to learn new material, just do some matching. Each aspect of inertia described earlier in this chapter—maintenance of direction and speed—correlate with two present-day realities wreaking havoc in our lives. (Maintenance of direction through fragmentation and multiple options, and maintenance of speed through data density and chaotic change.) What follows is an application of personal inertia to these realities—the *way* for the *will*; how you can *keep going* once you *get going*.

Maintenance of Direction through Fragmentation

The current *fragmentation* within society obstructs the traditional paths many travel throughout life. Even in the recent past, proactive approaches were not as necessary. Most people employed a reactive stance, making minor adjustments to prescribed routes. The inertia of large, established structures and institutions carried along the individual participants. In most families, a parent—or most likely a grandparent—can reminisce about a thirty-plus-year career with one company, a vocational experience that now has become extremely rare.

When these organizations began to fracture, the overall purpose of individuals' lives, intertwined within such institutions, hit a dead end. The heavy industrial orientation of the United States was splintering by virtue of globalization, technology, changes in financial management, and the transition to service industries. The repercussions fanned out into communities and families. Those who attempted to gain direction within the remnants created by this fragmentation often encountered continued fracturing of the pieces. With outside resources in such great flux, orientation points were lost, and the first signs of purpose paralysis surfaced.

An individual who is aware of personal inertia has convictions that can maintain a sense of direction throughout the ongoing fragmentation of historical structures. A proactive stance might be maintained even as known paths begin to splinter into smaller and smaller slivers. The density of such released convictions helps individuals continue to have motion even as the large institutional vehicles upon which many hitched a ride screech to a halt or explode into a thousand pieces. On the other hand, if an individual's beliefs, values, and personal maturity have never been inventoried and focused into personal convictions, the available orientation points are scattered and momentum is lost.

Maintenance of Direction Through Multiple Options

The need to focus our energies has become an enormous challenge. The *proliferation of options* creates new opportunities, but also can overload our ability to filter through them. The late 1990's saw the options explosion supersede reality in the ".com" fiasco. People launched companies with no products or services to sell, and investors jumped onboard so as not to miss what looked like great opportunities. Heralded as a new economy, it proved to be nothing more than the old economy attempting to embrace new technology without a sound foundation.

The appearance of a hot option truly may usher in a new opportunity, but individuals without clear direction often get burned. In regions prone to forest fires, especially during dry stretches, homeowners are encouraged to clean up the "slash" around their houses—all the debris that has accumulated around their property and can quickly become fuel for an advancing fire. Individuals also need to filter out some of the slash strewn around their lives, potential energy that can quickly ignite an out-of-control situation.

Identified convictions released under the influence of inertia and propelled into motion by passion can maintain consistent direction through all else that vies for our attention. Without convictions of substance, an individual's life reacts no longer like a cannonball but rather a ping-pong ball that bounces from side to side. A conviction may dictate openness to new opportunities, but if a suitable goal is not clearly defined, motion will be stalled by indecision. A multiple-option society mandates that we develop solid convictions and maintain consistent direction toward a well-defined goal, or we are doomed to a life of perpetual "channel surfing".

Maintenance of Speed through Data Density

The second aspect of inertia highlighted in this chapter, *maintenance of speed*, can be matched with *data density* and *chaotic change*. Each day we must process the ever-growing mountain of information whipped by the fickle winds of change.

Debates rage about the rate at which we generate data today. Analysts say it would require just half a decade and possibly less to produce an amount of new information to match the level of the entire last century. No one argues that the rate at which information is now generated is both fast and overwhelming. The sheer weight of knowledge available to us overpowers the processing abilities of mere human beings. Supposedly, only a small portion of brain potential is utilized. In years to come, more neurons and synapses may take up the slack and allow increased mental processing and storage. In the meantime, the current glut of information can slow our ability to analyze and deduce clear, appropriate life direction.

The amount of information opens many new frontiers, but also creates crossroads at which a growing number of signs point confusingly in various directions. The struggle to process all possible needs and options causes many people to stop dead in their tracks, unable to choose a definite direction in which to proceed. In such a case, an overload can trip our mental circuit breakers and precipitate a shutdown of all systems.

Another common response is to dilute the density of our convictions by absorbing an overflow of data. The result is Styrofoam®, a loose conglomeration of interests and possibilities that do not deliver a high level of impact.

Firm convictions that maintain speed through the haze and debris of data prevent a life from stalling from information overload. Convictions set into action with momentum toward a clearly defined goal can allow for useful additions to one's information base, while also bypassing what is not essentially useful. The effort committed to identifying convictions with substance lays the blueprint for future evaluation of data and separation of the essential from the nonessential. This work of prioritizing does not discount vast amounts of potentially useful information as useless; rather, it provides a track on which to maintain motion.

Maintenance of Speed through Chaotic Change

The maintenance of speed prevents an individual from becoming bogged down with information. It also allows for *maintenance of pace* even as *the rate of change* around us continues to accelerate. This final application of the two aspects of inertia highlighted in this chapter responds to a critical dilemma created by modern life. Existence in contemporary society demands that we live at a pace that becomes unsustainable. The rate of change infiltrates and influences the previous three dynamics of contemporary culture we have mentioned: *fragmentation, increased options,* and *data overload.* These three unfold at breakneck speed.

It is relatively easy to understand how these first three realities give a push to the tempo of modern-day life. Viewed from any of these perspectives, the consequence remains the same: a pace of life set at a level few can maintain. As most of us can well see, a person living life at full throttle will need to take a break or will simply hit the wall.

The created order described in the Old Testament of the Bible allowed a break in the tempo, a time for rest. Weekly Sabbath allowed refreshment from a week of labor, but the original commandment to observe periods of rest went even further. The land was to rest from production in defined cycles. A respite from loans and indenturing was detailed in the Year of Jubilee. These precautions helped maintain a manageable pace for life on a number of levels. The toll brought on by physical labor for mere survival was high, but the pace of life remained at a predictable and reasonable intensity. Individuals who adhere to the principle of Sabbath rest can affirm that it brings them clarity of purpose enhanced by reserves of energy.

Yet the preservation of balance within human life is rarely encouraged. The current challenge more often comes, not from the toil of physical labor, but from the toil of our attempts to keep up with life lived at an unsustainable pace. Balance is obliterated by fear of falling behind. The inevitable result is a period of frenetic activity followed by succumbing to the ravages of life lived at an unbearable pace.

Trained to Go the Distance

This aspect of inertia—maintenance of speed—allows individuals to retain balance in what has become an unbalanced world. At a time when many burn out and check out, this incredible natural asset is available to all. Nature provides a built-in governor.

Recall the individuals you may have known who scoffed at the importance of a reasonable pace and balance. More likely than not, they have moved to another company; had an emotional, physical, or moral breakdown; developed an addiction; and/or disappeared and have never been heard from again. Solid convictions spur the release of actions that are released under the influence of inertia, and will proceed at the pace at which they are set in motion. Increased speed is sometimes required to deliver impact; but the sensible maintenance of velocity at other appropriate times allows for continual motion that assures a more sustainable pace.

Desired Orderliness and Balance

Maintenance of direction and speed, matched to challenges of life in the twenty-first century, provide orderliness and balance in an environment with increased disorder and imbalance. This holds true even in today's atmosphere, replete with fragments of traditional institutions, a meteor shower of information, and black holes of options, all accelerated to the speed of light. This truth of motion can provide us with a path through the chaos of contemporary life, and the opportunity to go with a flow that nature provides.

A focused and efficient vision for one's life is necessary for survival in an era that has replaced the traditional pursuits of purpose with the need for a proactive mission. Present-day dynamics no longer provide the opportunity of going with the flow without conscious effort. For many of us, it appears that debris has dammed the flow. In response, individuals must develop a means to navigate through life, aware of what nature still has to offer that enables us to deliver with impact.

The Third Aspect

There is a third aspect of inertia that accentuates the possibility of a narrow, precise focus: *the tendency of objects in motion to move in a straight line.* In the next chapter, we will add this quintessential component to the development of a life of impact as we continue to uncover the *way* for the *will.*

Questions

Chapter Four

1. Record everyday physical examples of aspects of inertia (maintenance of direction and speed).

2. Considering the universe as a unified whole, what relationships have you observed between physical realities and your life? (Recall the following examples: phases of the moon, the presence of sunlight.)

3. One aspect of the *way* presented in this chapter, maintenance of direction, allows for movement through present-day fragmentation and the proliferation of options. What might this look like in your life?

4. The second aspect of the *way*, maintenance of speed, allows for movement through the information explosion and the accelerated rate of change. What might this look like in your life?

5. Which of the two aspects presented is most needed in your life?

CHAPTER FIVE

Follow the Direct Route

"As the crow flies."
"The shortest distance between two points is a straight line."

A well-known story involves the installation of sidewalks on college campuses. For years, new buildings had been constructed and landscaped with pre-designed walkways that accentuated the overall campus aesthetics. The problem with this approach was that the students did not use the paved walks. Instead, paths that represented the shortest routes to the new facilities developed in the newly laid sod. The story ends with an obvious solution to this landscaping dilemma. At some universities, when a new building is constructed and opened, the sidewalks are poured after the students have had the opportunity to beat a path that represents the straightest line to the new facility. This example most likely represents an innate grasp of efficiency of motion, rather than a display of the mastery of geometry. Yet on our own life journeys, we easily wander off in various directions, ending up on a detour from a life of impact.

A general lack of enthusiasm and overall sense of dread can attest to some major roadblocks, or detours, in your life journey. A favorite family vacation story recounts what is now referred to as the Wyoming Detour. While traveling on a major state road, signs alerted to upcoming road construction and a detour—not a pleasant thought when visiting an unfamiliar region. What we discovered as we approached this work zone was that the pavement had been completely removed and the detour was a drive through a field! Has your life gotten off track and ended up far afield?

The Third Aspect

The examples above illustrate a third aspect of the universal law of motion that constitutes inertia, *the tendency of objects to move in a straight line.* Returning to our example outside the confines of Earth's gravity and atmosphere, we are once again able to utilize the Styrofoam® ball and cannonball that have become our familiar object lessons. If both balls were released into the vastness of space with the same initial acceleration, they would maintain direction and speed, and also travel in a straight line in the weightless environment. They do not execute loops or zigzags; they travel a straight path. The natural order of the universe incorporates an economy of motion.

The Efficient Way

After uncovering in Part One what matters to us—the force of our convictions—we can discover what keeps us moving with the shortest-distance focus toward our conviction-driven goals. In Part Two we continue to discover the *way* for the *will*—a *way* that is both consistent and efficient. Chapter Four explored two aspects of inertia that relate to *consistency* of motion: direction and speed. This chapter will now examine a third aspect of inertia that expresses *efficiency* of motion.

The previous example demonstrated the efficiency of motion, the tendency to move in a straight line in the weightless vacuum of space. Now let's consider earthbound examples of objects tending to proceed in a straight line.

When a projectile is fired from a gun, its speed is diminished as an effect of and in proportion to resistance from the earth's atmosphere and gravity. But its direction and its tendency to travel in a straight line remain true if the projectile is released at a high velocity in relation to its mass and density. The bullet does not waver from the course on which it was released.

If you are a runner who has participated in a 10K race, you know well this last aspect of inertia. During the first couple of kilometers you enjoy your surroundings, not even cognizant of your big looping turns. But if you are striving for a certain finish time, when the kilometers start to add up, you become fixated on your efficiency of motion, not wanting to take an unnecessary step. If you accidentally step in front of another runner you might hear how critical the shortest distance between two points has become to some participants!

Building the Model

This reality of the universe increasingly blurs in the chaotic race of life, creating a variety of detours on the path to impact. Chapter Four explored how the natural order promotes consistency of motion in the face of dynamics that contribute to inconsistency. Now we'll explore how personal inertia encourages efficiency in the midst of inefficiency.

We seem to be on an incessant search for the ultimate short cut. Techniques and products continually appear on the scene in response to this need. Several years ago a book that captured the theme of greater efficiency became popular: *The One Minute Manager* by Ken Blanchard.[23] Other strategies for organizations have also arisen, including the "flattening" of administrative structures to facilitate communication and decision making, computer networking within companies, and the advent of cell phones, Palm Pilots and Blackberries. The ultimate in modern efficiency is now available: devices that combine a number of functions into one item.

Purposeful Efficiency

The dynamics of inertia operate in a matrix of daily life that becomes ever more chaotic. While cues exist, the natural order blurs over time. Technologies and techniques meant to assist threaten to inundate and overtake—an indication of why so many suffer from paralysis of purpose.

Consider the growing list of detours that divert the *way* for your *will*: redefinition of work, technology obsession, regional economic shifts, a myriad of global factors, and the volume of information, to name a few.

Efficiency in this context implies not adding to, but rather clearing away—the conscious removal of what resists, sidetracks, and clutters the natural desire and tendency to take a straight line in life. In a passage from the Old Testament of the Bible, also quoted in all four Gospels of the New Testament, the prophet Isaiah speaks of clearing a straight path for the Messiah. The most efficient route needed to be created for the one that came to restore. It is recorded in the Gospel of Matthew, "For this is He who was spoken of by the prophet Isaiah when he said, '...the voice of one calling in the wilderness: Prepare the way of the Lord, make His paths straight.'" (Matthew 3:3 RSV) The theory of *life momentum* built on personal inertia is about the restoration of the straight route for that which brings a new sense of purpose.

Staying on Course

Restoration of the straight route in life requires continual course corrections. A measure of control is required. A natural dynamic of personal inertia is to maintain a straight line, but a clear target is necessary to maximize the impact.

The book *Lost Moon* by astronaut Jim Lovell (and the movie, *Apollo 13*, subsequently made from it) illustrates the incredible ability of individuals to overcome long odds through clear focus and passion motivated by survival. At one point in the story, a course correction was necessary, but the computer had been turned off earlier to conserve battery power. The astronauts needed a fixed point to provide orientation to execute the rocket burn necessary to keep them on target with a correct reentry trajectory. In a rather ironic twist, Lovell used the earth as his fixed point and attempted to keep his view of the earth in the center of the space capsule's window. In this case, the ultimate destination was also the orientation point along the way. [24]

With our ultimate goal (a life of impact) in the center of the window, what can help facilitate course corrections? What strategies can help us make adjustments that maximize nature's desire for an efficiency of motion and keep us on our journeys?

Basic Needs To Stay On Course

Personal Mission Statement. What a person keeps "in the window" is of critical importance. In what arenas does an individual desire to create the high impact we've mentioned so frequently? To what end are the aspects of inertia—maintenance of speed in a single, straight-line direction—employed?

The interior examination in Chapter One established what can be placed in motion—convictions with density, or substance, that have the potential to build the highest levels of inertial momentum. Convictions are built on beliefs and values distilled by personal maturity. But there remains the need to establish the realization of what a particular conviction will look like in "real time." The lack of a clearly defined destination will not allow for maximum utilization of inertial dynamics.

A succinctly delineated, personal mission statement is necessary for the highest impact potential. With this target, course adjustments take place in the service of the mission. The impact of the initial conviction becomes obvious over time. Detours can be avoided.

Talk of a mission can suggest the idea of acting through religious faith. Widely used today in a variety of contexts, the concept of a mission still holds a faith-based connotation for a number of people. Consider the progression from initial beliefs to personal impact through the words of Jesus. Jesus summarized the Ten Commandments and additional Old Testament laws in this manner: "You shall love the Lord your God with all your heart, and with all your soul, and with all your mind....You shall love your neighbor as yourself" (Matthew 22:37b and 39b RSV).

These two summaries are a synthesis of fundamental beliefs that create convictions. But what specifically is the target, and how will impact be determined? The latitude in these two statements has allowed organized religion at times to veer off course through the lack of a specific statement of mission.

Jesus addressed what contributed to the development of the mission:

> Then the King will say to those at his right hand, "Come, O blessed of my Father, inherit the kingdom prepared for you from the foundation of the world; for I was hungry and you gave me

food, I was thirsty and you gave me drink, I was a stranger and you welcomed me, I was naked and you clothed me, I was sick and you visited me, I was in prison and you came to me." Then the righteous will answer him, "Lord, when did we see thee hungry and feed thee...?" And the King will answer them, "Truly, I say to you, as you did it to one of the least of these my brethren, you did it to me." (Matthew 25:34–37a, 40 RSV)

Personal Competencies. The interior life inventory in Chapter One challenges individuals to take a wide-angle look at their lives. This view takes into consideration the whole person's development; what one is made of together with what one hopes to accomplish. The business world is quite familiar with this type of evaluation: a complete look at the individual, measured not just against productivity, but also against the competencies necessary to improve performance on a number of levels. General competencies are assumed for all employees, but particular positions will mandate specific competencies and attainment of a higher degree of growth.

Why revisit this after one's mission is clearly defined? When concerned with course correction, an important task relates to the specific competencies required to realize a particular mission. A lack of these competencies does not allow for sustained motion toward the goal. Competencies serve as signs along the way that allow your will to stay on course toward your conviction-driven mission.

Consider the example of establishing a mentoring program. To maintain a shortest-distance focus assisted by the natural order, a couple of unique competencies keep this conviction and subsequent mission statement on track and rolling along: *knowledge* of the inner workings of particular schools and the school system in general, and *expertise* in the available models and materials utilized in other settings. This is the

David and Kenneth Smazik

difference between knowing whom to approach with which program design and driving to the closest elementary school and announcing to an overworked administrative assistant that you have arrived to impact society by mentoring kids. It is not unrealistic to require that for each conviction identified, the necessary competencies are also identified and developed to assist the motion, to keep one's pursuit of purpose on the straightest possible line.

The Shortest-Distance Focus for the Will

Chapters Four and Five combine to delineate what the perspective of personal inertia recognizes as a shortest-distance focus of consistency and efficiency. Convictions that gain assistance from natural inertial tendencies are not thrown off course onto detours when clear mission statements and competencies provide guidance. We are able to maintain a straight-line efficiency throughout our day-to-day lives. The *way* has been revealed to plot our life course with assistance from the natural contours, or dynamics, of the universe. We **can** gain and maintain life momentum toward meaningful impact at a time when others see no discernible path, let alone a direct route, for their *will*.

Questions

Chapter Five

1. "The shortest distance between two points is a straight line." When has this third aspect of inertia been exhibited in your life?

2. What would your personal mission statement contain? What is the target for your life (realized convictions)?

3. What additional competencies might you need?

4. Consider the ways you have not utilized the reality of inertia: objects in motion maintain their speed and direction in a straight line.

CHAPTER SIX

Restart when Stalled

"You're like a bump on a log!"
"Get with the program!"
"I'll start tomorrow."

This book has been all about motion, but our frustration level may continue to grow because we feel destined to remain stuck in neutral. Life at the start of a new millennium has become a maze of fractured structures, options, and information, much like a spaghetti-bowl highway interchange. Opportunities open and close at an increasingly fast pace. The dynamics that are helping to create the present world disorder have been documented. The combination of environmental and social sources, as well as internal, system-oriented sources, has created the debilitating strain of paralysis of purpose now so prevalent.

The good news is that inertia is present in life whether at rest or in motion. Remember, inertia is a neutral law of the universe that explains the maintenance of activity or inactivity. The bad news is that our inactivity is what inertia might currently maintain. Here's a common reminder of how difficult it can be to get going and keep going on our personal journeys. What's the status of that New Year's resolution to exercise daily? Every day can be a battle to carve out time and push our bodies to a level that will help our goals show in our waistlines. The natural inclination of most well-meaning people is not a lifetime membership at the local health club. Something pulls us back onto the couch. Realities of the universe give an assist to our persistent inactivity.

Earthbound Challenges

Three natural forces that stack the deck against motion, apart from current societal challenges, are homeostasis, gravity, and friction from the atmosphere. Translated into terms related to human activity, the cards also are stacked against placing identified convictions of substance into motion. This chapter examines the impact that two of the forces, homeostasis and gravity, exert in concert with the dynamic of inertia that maintains an object at rest, inactivity.

Natural Balance

Homeostasis. There is a natural balance that virtually all systems seek to maintain. It is a dynamic necessary to the healthy functioning and survival of the created order. Our environment must maintain a delicate balance to support an immense variety of plant and animal life. Homeostasis, a balance of systems, is present within each of the species that make up the plant and animal kingdoms in order for each organism to experience optimal health.

Human beings' diverse and intricate systems exhibit an exquisite balance. Respiratory and circulatory systems are two of those systems. These two network with a host of other systems, even as each system maintains its own internal homeostasis. Heart and lung functions are closely linked; the balance of red and white blood cells and oxygen dictates a close relationship between these organs. A deficiency in one of these major organs affects the other dramatically, and a ripple effect is experienced throughout the body's systems.

A Long History

The New Testament writer, Paul, used an ancient grasp of homeostasis as an illustration for the infant Christian church. When all the parts are present and coordinated with other systems, a healthy organization will exist. "For just as the body is one and has many members, all the members of the body, though many, are one body," he states. "For the body does not consist of one member but of many." (2 Corinthians 12:12 ab and 14 RSV)

In their book *Generation to Generation*, Strauss and Howe make a very impressive case for defined generational groups that have threaded their way through the history of the United States. What may appear as generational traits that spread a chaotic shroud over the landscape of a nation, Strauss and Howe uncover as clear patterns. The authors present examples of the action/reaction reality of nature, the desire to bring balance. One generation looks askance at authority and traditional conventions; the next appears to embrace tradition and often resemble their grandparents and even great-great grandparents in specific beliefs. A succeeding age group might eventually bridge what at first appeared to be a generation gap.[25]

Stacked Against Motion

When the dynamic of inertia that maintains an object at rest merges with the innate desire for homeostasis, we have a simple equation that adds up to the development of an entrenched "Comfort Zone." In this state of rest, individuals have no identified convictions or only a few interests that receive no push from personal passion. *Homeostasis is sought, and this static state is then maintained by inertia.* Life is lived from the Lay-Z-Boy with remote in hand. Rationalization and justification assist the balancing process and release a person from any personal responsibility. A rest stop during life's journey has become a permanent residence.

The presence of homeostasis and the dynamic of inertia that maintains objects at rest make it easier to detect why only a small percentage of individuals seem to journey toward conviction-driven goals.

What About Gravity?

Gravity. The reason it is difficult to initiate and sustain motion on earth is that we live under the effects of gravity. Objects are pulled toward the earth's center and held on the surface of the planet by the force of gravity. The weight of an object is a measure of this force. A cannonball fired with great velocity and initially able to break through a wall will eventually fall to the ground. Gravity is the reason that even objects with initial acceleration do not maintain their speed and direction in a straight line on Earth.

Manifestations of Situational Gravity

In our personal efforts, when we attempt to "get the lead out," there is often an apparent force that pulls us down and holds us in place. Consider factors that are a situation of birth: race, religion, economic resources, region of world, and status of family. These factors, for the majority of the world's population, have traditionally held an individual in "place." The caste culture in India may be the most blatant example of both situational gravity and societal homeostasis, but similar realities exist in all cultures.

Consider two applicants for an executive position at a corporate New York office. One applicant of average intelligence and motivation comes from an Eastern family, who for many generations attended a particular Ivy League school and whose family name can be recognized from industry and regional politics. Another applicant, an extremely bright individual with exceptional drive, is a second generation American from a small town in the Midwest who attended the local college. It is a common assumption that status of family will win out in the hiring process.

Varying degrees of situational gravity have a hold on most lives. Common phrases express this reality: "Looking for the big break"; "It's not what you know but who you know"; "It's all a matter of timing." Each one of these statements implies development of motion and release from a present situation.

Situational gravity can also exert its grip in contemporary society by more subtle means. The fallout from the technology explosion has affected many lives, creating a hold on their progress. Individuals affected by downsizing and replaced by new technology; older workers replaced by those raised on computers; and the outsourcing of jobs to countries now connected through various technologies to our own. A call for technological assistance might literally be answered from the other side of the world.

Many factors may increase the potency of gravity within a life and on the subsequent presence of homeostasis. To state that the dynamic of inertia is a reality, without recognizing other factors that aid in maintaining inaction, would not accurately portray the challenge that confronts people who long for lives of impact. The natural pull of gravity and subsequent leveling or balance seeking within this state can highlight the desire for the comfort level inherent in this condition. We may think something isn't quite right, but we can't put our fingers on what that *something* is. Our lives are in neutral. We have stalled out. The natural laws of the universe are at work, but the initiation and sustainability of motion toward purpose and subsequent impact has never quite been realized.

It's Still Holding Us Back

On both the physical and metaphysical planes, a reality of earthbound existence is the need to overcome the pull of gravity—a pull that appears to increase as the forces of disorder whirl around us at an ever-increasing pace. For the bicycle, motor vehicle, or airplane that sits quietly on the earth's surface, a push or impetus is necessary to overcome the pull of gravity and initiate motion. If the fuel supply runs out, motion can be maintained for a brief period because of inertial principles, but gravity will prevail.

Most of us desire to be in the best possible physical condition, but if our enthusiasm toward exercise wanes, our physical fitness programs fizzle. The same is true if no effort is applied to the recognition and development of the emotional life; no progress is made, even with the passage of years. With no commitment to improve needed competencies for the workplace, and with a belief that the deficiency is outside the individual, nothing will change in terms of performance. New attitudes toward others might be desired, but with no attention to spiritual growth, the old negative attitudes can progress even further into hostility. We have created a variety of comfort zones that gravity now holds in place.

Reframing Our Perspective

The presence of gravity, homeostasis, and inertia do not conspire to work against the pursuit of purpose; *they exist in a neutral state.* We need a new *perspective.* Recall the stereographic image of a three-dimensional figure hidden in the mosaic of a thousand splotches of color. Nothing additional is required for perception of the imbedded image except a new perspective. The need to take a fresh look at these universal realities is the challenge, much like a skilled photographer snapping at just the right moment to capture the unique perspective.

The thoughts and work of *National Geographic* photographer Dewitt Jones is the basis for a helpful leadership/business training video. This presentation is powerful because of the fresh perspective of its images. Many of us have attempted to take a photo, but with a new approach to the exact same scene, one can discover a completely new perspective.

[For Your Consideration]

- Creativity is a matter of perspective.
- There's always more than one right answer.
- Reframe problems into opportunities.
- Don't be afraid to make mistakes.
- Break the pattern.
- Train your technique.
- You've really got to care.[26]

Each person has the potential to see new possibilities in what has always been there before. The natural laws that have maintained inaction can maintain motion. *Homeostasis in a life of inactivity can convert to a state of balance within a life of forward progress.* The same elements are present, but a new image of life has emerged.

Let Personal Passion Break This Full-Life Hold

There is fuel that can help us accelerate sufficiently in order to overcome gravity and experience motion-maintaining dynamics of inertia to build life momentum. Without clear knowledge of what is important the needed form of propulsion or motivation remains elusive.

What are you attempting to place into motion? In the history of aviation, pedaling by foot was attempted as a means of getting a flying machine airborne. There is ample photographic evidence that this method was not appropriate to achieving the desire of humanity to fly. When this miscalculation became inescapably apparent, alternate means of propulsion were used successfully. Once convictions are identified, the emphasis turns to the appropriate impetus for both initial liftoff and sustainability.

In Chapter Two, the label *personal passion* was applied to the impetus necessary to propel identified convictions. Examples of the power of high-octane passion illustrated its effectiveness. High-performance fuels achieve their status through a process of refinement. In order to overpower the force of gravity consistently within a life, a continual refinement of passion is necessary.

The Need for Discipline vs. A "Lottery Mentality"

Without the presence of personal discipline, passion lacks its maximum power; thus, identified convictions lack sufficient propulsion acceleration, and there is no opportunity for inertia to build and maintain motion, speed, and direction in a straight line. The bottom line is there is no life impact due to situational gravity, holding us down.

This book has presented multiple nuances of life that contribute to the present universal sense of disorder and unpredictability. In light of the incredible odds against the development of motivating passion refined by discipline, gravity clearly has the upper hand.

It almost appears that there is a conspiracy in place, mitigating against anything to do with discipline. Recall the effort to regularly jog or walk for exercise. Instant gratification appears to be winning the day. Consider the numerous marketed products that speak to the pervasive contemporary philosophy of instant gratification—all the way from weight loss *(Have the perfect body in three weeks!)* to investment opportunities, to the possibility of acquiring advanced degrees without effort or study. This is just a small sample of the ubiquitous advertising messages that claim we can have it all right now. It becomes a lottery mentality: Buy just one ticket, and have no worries for the rest of your life.

The development of passion, the accelerant for our convictions of substance, involves discipline. There are no shortcuts to physical, intellectual, emotional, vocational, or spiritual development. Minimal effort results in minuscule velocity for our convictions. The structure and routine of discipline develops strength and power within our lives. Daily exercise keeps muscles and various systems of the body well toned. A weekly schedule of reading keeps your intellect fine-tuned. Consistent intentional contact with family and friends promotes emotional health.

Philosopher and theologian Dallas Willard writes in his book *The Spirit of the Disciplines* that Jesus exhibited a distinct commitment to discipline, including time spent apart from others for meditation, prayer, and study.[27] Willard states that discipline places a person in a position to effectively confront the challenges that will inevitably come in life. Without appropriate disciplines toning our passion, a life may remain stalled; it might never lift off the ground or out of the rut. If by chance it becomes airborne, the flight will typically be short.

Try Again to Put the Pieces in Place

The experience of being stuck, having difficulty getting started, highlights one principle of inertia: that objects at rest will remain in this state unless propelled by a motivating force. Other laws of the universe also contribute to this condition of inactivity, including gravity and homeostasis. A new perspective, and an accelerant, passion refined through discipline, is necessary to initiate motion. The result is motion that—in spite of the pervasive dynamics of the present world disorder—maintains speed and direction in a straight line. Such motion maintains its inertial properties, powering through obstacles that threaten to throw a life off course. At a time when so many of the traditional orientation points have been obscured and many wander aimlessly, a *clearly delineated focus* is both necessary and possible.

With the force of convictions of substance and an unencumbered focus, we now confront that which impedes motion head-on: *friction from resistance*. We will examine what slows you down when in motion and how to develop what we term *least-resistance living*.

Questions

Chapter Six

1. Can you list your last set of New Year's resolutions? Does your continual inactivity cause a high level of frustration?

2. How has your life established comfort (balance or homeostasis) around inactivity?

3. What pulls your life down (gravity), impeding progress toward impact?

4. Develop a list of disciplines that would give full expression to your passion, the needed acceleration for your convictions.

5. Within your present life context, how would the force of convictions (Part One), combined with the aspects of inertia (Part Two), direction, speed and straight line efficiency, help you to get going and keep going?

PART THREE

Discover What Slows You Down

CHAPTER SEVEN

Signs of Wear and Tear

"The heat's on!"
"I could just scream!"
"I jumped from the frying pan right into the fire!"

Without an awareness of various forms of resistance that create friction, even convictions of substance placed in motion can fall short of their destinations. Momentum is lost. These universal forms of friction are expressed uniquely in our lives and are in addition to present day challenges shared in Part II. To identify the kinds of collisions that can take place between convictions and various elements in a particular atmosphere, we return to examples in specific arenas of life.

I Sense Some Friction!

Family. For a parent, an identified conviction can be the focus on family through growing relationships. The conviction itself is in order, founded on core beliefs and values, and filtered through personal maturity. In this case, the placement of the conviction into motion meets considerable resistance, equivalent to a wall, from a rebellious teenager. Resistance is built to a level that creates enough friction to halt the forward motion of the conviction. This barrier to impact is the type of resistance that infiltrates the entire atmosphere within the home and results in heated exchanges.

Vocation. For another individual, an identified conviction is the clear and open sharing of information in the workplace. The placement of this conviction into motion remains partial until there is resolution of a recurring disconnect that impedes interoffice communication and impacts the effectiveness of the sales force. The resistance in this atmosphere comes from two individuals who will share only a bare minimum of information, therefore, creating a high level of friction. The amount of friction does not stall the movement of the initial conviction completely, but it greatly impedes its motion, and is manifested in groans of frustration.

Community. A small group of local citizens band together around the conviction that affordable housing should be available to all. Multiple forms of resistance from a number of other organizations impede its motion. The atmosphere is thick with resistance to the small group's passion to purchase a downtown building and begin repairs. The conviction of this small group needs implementation through a completely different form due to the almost complete breakdown of this dream.

When friction is present within a life, the energy available to maintain motion of convictions toward impact is converted into another form, reducing the available amount for realization of one's purpose. The forms into which the presence of friction (resistance) converts the energy of motion are *heat, noise,* and *material breakdown.* If we make the effort to identify these components in our lives we will discover the ineffective use of our limited energy, the *resistance* that impedes and/or completely stops the *way* of the *will*.

So, how do we commit the amount of energy we possess in our lives? More specifically, how do we reconvert the energy consumed by friction to help generate the forward motion of our convictions?

The Basic Manifestations of Friction

A cord woven through this book relates to the total-life reality of truths that are often defined as physical realities. An obvious manner in which this cord wraps itself in and around our lives is the manifestation of friction. The commonality is remarkable, whether the brakes are applied to a vehicle or to the realization of conviction-driven goals.

Applied over time, the friction from brake pads disrupting the motion of the tires on a vehicle will convert the energy of the motion into **heat**. Mere proximity to brakes after a trip through stop and go traffic is enough to allow one to feel the heat. When friction continues over a period of time, the chirping or screeching **noise** from use of our brakes alerts a driver to the wear from excessive friction. A bill of sale for parts and labor from the local mechanic confirms the **material breakdown** of these parts because of the energy that has been converted.

The similarity of manifestations of friction within a life is uncanny. When your desire to proceed to a destination is thwarted by another driver cutting you off, the elevation of your heart rate brought on by anger and frustration causes you to feel hot, just as the slamming of your brakes causes the various components to heat up quickly. If the same person appears to target you for a blocking maneuver a second time, as your brakes screech, you may scream a few remarks in protest. If this behavior persists, you will soon have had it—*road rage* may show its ugly head. You might want to leave a lasting impression on this irritating driver. The integrity of your braking system and of your character are both at the breaking point.To identify the presence of friction that converts and diverts the energy of your convictions in motion, *search in those places where you detect the heat of anger, or groans of frustration, or where your integrity breaks down.*

Heat

When the limited amount of energy you possess is converted to forms of "heat," that same energy is diverted from its potential to help power a life of impact. Expressions of anger are reportedly on the rise. You might admit that anger surfaces quickly when you're confronting a less-than-helpful store clerk, or when you finally talk to a real person on the phone after a trip through several electronic options. Road rage, rage expressed by parents at youth sporting events, the rage of unruly passengers aboard airplanes, and the rage released in acts of violence in schools are some examples of a pervasive and growing nationwide trend.

The heat of anger alerts an individual to the presence of one or more areas of friction within a life. Anger can serve as an indicator of wasted resources in your life, well before an unappeasable rage consumes all the natural resources you possess.

Noise

Groans, grimaces, and other sometimes more literal "noises" of frustration also are on the rise in the atmosphere of contemporary life. The effective person, or person of conviction, traces noise caused by frustration to the friction that creates these feelings of irritation. The recognition and reduction of this recurring friction allows an individual to maintain their cumulative frustration at a level that uses a lower amount of valuable energy.

Breakdown of Structural Integrity

The persistent presence of friction, and especially extremely high levels of friction, invariably causes the irreversible breakdown of the materials involved. This situation is often referred to as a compromise of the basic structural integrity of a material. The continual presence of a high level of friction within a life has the same effect: the breakdown of structural integrity. The breakdown of integrity may express itself in various ways, including actions contrary to core beliefs and values, actions that exhibit a low level of emotional and spiritual development, or activities that represent an attempt to escape from present circumstances through an addiction or a continual need of extreme experiences.

When the structural integrity of components that comprise any mechanical device are compromised by extreme or relentless friction, it is time to visit the repair shop for an overhaul. Similarly, when an individual experiences a breakdown of integrity, a time of serious evaluation is necessary. Friction that has converted enough energy to cause a breakdown needs identification, along with the internal systems that have yielded to this pressure.

A Winning Perspective

Effective coaches, managers, teachers, pastors, or directors of nonprofit organizations, seem to know intuitively that people have a limited amount of energy with which to work. This group instinctively observes and responds to obvious manifestations of heat, noise, and structural breakdowns. It is a reality of our daily lives, yet one that most people do not take time to quantify. The ability to assist people in focusing and maximizing their energies to sustain motion toward a goal separates those who are consistently effective and those who are not.

Phil Jackson, former head coach of the Chicago Bulls and the Los Angeles Lakers, is credited with reducing the distractions that swirl around NBA superstars and instilling a focus on the fundamentals of basketball—even convincing megawatt superstars that a good pass is as important as a spectacular dunk. Christian Majgarrd, CEO of LEGO, states this same truth in another manner: "What I learned was that the business system must facilitate, not impede, the flow and refinement of ideas so that they can be realized."[28]

A master teacher reduces the distraction of a growing list of life concerns that compete for a student's attention, and instead draws the pupil into a learning environment that captivates all the energies available for comprehension. The effective pastor identifies and mitigates the multiple forms of friction that threaten to subvert the relatively small amounts of energy most individuals are willing to commit to a faith community.

The above samples of life scenarios are common in the increasing disorder in all realms of modern life. The potential types of resistance that can impede a life and create friction are expanding at an incredible rate of speed. Failure to understand that there is a limited reservoir of energy within a person's life can doom an individual to immobility.

Even effective coaches, managers, teachers, and pastors are mystified by their own results. Many do not believe they possess exceptional intelligence or unique abilities. What they do possess is the understanding that the reduction and elimination of friction within a life allows for the unimpeded motion from productive energy, passion, as well as the possibility to *get on a roll* and build momentum for individuals and often for organizations.

What To Look For

All of us know well the heat of anger when progress toward a goal is thwarted, the sound of frustration when motion is slowed or inhibited, and the breakdown of structural integrity when friction persists. The basic ideas presented in this chapter assist a person in identifying the outward manifestations of resistance that impede progress toward a life of impact. A critical measurement often ignored is the total amount of energy each person possesses for the pursuit of life goals. *This reservoir of energy already exists within everyone and is either released as passion accelerating identified convictions or is converted by friction to nonproductive uses that impede or stall momentum in our lives.*

We have raised our level of awareness to the presence of friction in our lives, and the forms into which this friction converts our limited supply of energy. We now can attack the specific types of friction draining our resources.

Questions

Chapter Seven

1. Record various examples of expended energy in your life, dispersed among a number of interests.

2. List how the following manifestations of friction exist in your personal world.
   - Anger/Bitterness (Heat):
   - Sounds of Frustration (Noise):
   - Lapses of Integrity (Breakdown of Material):

3. What continues to wear on your life, creating paralysis of motion toward purpose?

CHAPTER EIGHT

Reduction of Friction

"We seem to have ground to a screeching halt."
"Who is putting on the brakes?"
"I didn't know what I was walking into."

When energy is diverted from passion about a conviction and is expressed in one of three forms—heat, noise, or material breakdown--we are alerted to the existence of one or more forms of friction within our lives. The presence and subsequent reduction of friction determines which convictions experience maintenance of motion and become habitual and which encounter resistance that impedes their progress.

We may have an awareness of our present predicament, acknowledge a high level of friction that burns valuable energy, but need more reference points. *What is the root cause of our thwarted progress and depleted energy?*

The running of a marathon is a microcosm of a life journey. There are considerable resistances that must be worked through to complete this race. We cannot continually have collisions with other runners, or any hope of finishing will be dashed. We don't want to be slowed down along the way from improper clothing or drag on our progress. And we must be in the best shape possible to even consider a run of this distance in the first place. This simple example displays three major forms of friction we all encounter throughout life.

Go To The Source

As we describe major forms of friction created by resistance in various situations, remember the key discoveries from Part One: The effects of resistance and the subsequent friction are greatly minimized by the density of one's convictions and the force of passion by which they are motivated, the level of inertia or momentum that has been created.

The presence of friction is not an inherent deterrent to discovering a life of impact. Like other universal realities—inertia, gravity, or homeostasis, for example—friction exists in what is best described as a state of neutrality. The properties of these laws do not make decisions whether to assist the motion of life toward purpose or to impede progress. That is for us to do, using an awareness of the application of these realities.

Sliding/Kinetic Friction

Kinetic friction is direct, head-on resistance to movement in a particular direction. Consider the task of moving a stationary box along the floor. Eventually, as one pushes harder and harder, the box slides. The box will continue to slide across the floor as long as the force you apply exceeds the sliding friction that resists movement.

It is easily learned that the amount of sliding friction depends on the weight of the object one is trying to move and the type of surface it rests on. It is much easier to push a light box on a slick surface than a heavy box on a rough surface. The rougher the terrain we need to traverse, the more resistance we will encounter. Likewise, the greater the magnitude of what we want to accomplish, the more head-on resistance we will likely encounter.

Consider the friction present in a century-old mainline denominational church. Based on an identified conviction of substance, a new idea is presented—an idea meant to sustain the church body through the current world disorder. What will it take to push this idea through? How can the resistance encountered be identified and placed into an appropriate perspective? The history of this group, and the various relationships similar to a family, have created a landscape that will require a high level of force with which to plow through. The person who presented the idea, typically the pastor, encounters entrenched, past tradition, represented and protected by one or more individuals resistant to any change, and is met with head-on resistance.

Minor resistance creates a negligible level of friction, but can quickly expand into a significant amount of sliding friction, creating a standoff between individuals and convictions. Consider how often progress is slowed in our life journeys due to a difference of opinion. Often a minor issue is built into something major that can become a force applied in the opposite direction.

Rolling Friction

This form of friction is defined as the force that impedes the progress of a rolling object. A brake pad that creates resistance when applied against a rolling wheel produces rolling friction. The degree of resistance and level of rolling friction created may slow a vehicle or can potentially bring it to a complete stop. If our well-worn Styrofoam® ball and cannonball were pushed with the same velocity on a flat surface, they would both encounter resistance from the atmosphere and from the surface as rolling friction, and come to a halt. The density of the cannonball would allow for a longer period of motion, but it, too, would eventually grind to a halt through the effects of rolling friction. That which impedes momentum and resists the motion or flow developed is considered rolling friction.

Consider a company which begins to get on a roll, to build some momentum. Their research and development department has hit on an ingenious design, the sales force is energized, and customers respond not only with orders but also with word-of-mouth endorsements. The momentum is present; the level of inertia builds speed and direction in a straight line to increased profits.

This momentum can only maintain itself through teamwork that requires clear and open communication among all departments. The general manager has great passion behind this identified conviction of open and clear communication, an obvious contribution to the current momentum. But the first signs of resistance are evident at a staff meeting; two department heads have chosen not to share all information in a clear and open manner. Each of them closely holds information, and the temperature in the room rises. Apparently, they view pieces of pertinent information as bargaining chips—a means of leverage for their own departments—or possibly they enjoy the illusion of power withholding information brings to their egos. The result of this appearance of resistance (through the action or inaction of two department heads concerning the general manager's convictions) creates friction, and the momentum of the entire company experiences the resistance.

The book *Promoting Emotional Intelligence in Organizations* by Cary Cherniss and Mitchell Adler describes a competency or "emotion" that has become ever more important: "One emotion that is particularly helpful for superior performance is flow...."[29] The example above illustrates the importance of individual and teams of employees developing this competency. Often the first evidence of rolling friction appears around a misunderstanding or resistance to *flow* toward the desired target. In our example, open and direct communication is the conviction; the desired activity is communication in consideration of the *flow,* or momentum.

Fluid Friction

This form of friction refers to the amount of *drag* on an object caused by numerous variables such as shape, material, speed, and viscosity. Fluid friction places greater emphasis on the design and environment of the object involved. A flat-bottom boat constructed of a rough material, powered by a twenty-five-horsepower engine, trolling murky backwaters will encounter more drag, or friction, than a bullet boat, powered by twin one-hundred-fifty-horsepower engines on a clear lake.

The example in Chapter Seven that first presented fluid friction described a small group of citizens attempting to respond to a community problem. An individual or, in the example presented, a group of individuals may have an identified conviction of substance with a high level of passion. The desired impact would have a pervasive effect on individuals able to get off the street or out of shelters and possess their own living spaces. As mentioned, this conviction encountered tremendous resistance from the start, and was never able to build inertia: resistance from governmental bodies in the form of endless paperwork and countless mandatory codes, funding sources supporting only portions of this concept, and local agencies wanting varying levels of involvement.

The initial design of a conviction, and analysis of the environment in which an individual or group of individuals will attempt to gain motion requires considerable evaluation. Beyond an obstacle that moves in direct opposition, or brakes that slow momentum, some convictions or ideas just won't float or cut through a particular atmosphere because of initial design flaws. Universal laws of aerodynamics are at work, whether in the water, on the ground, or in the air. Each environment consists of a unique resistance that requires specific design modifications.

A form of fluid friction is often found in the atmosphere of a mainline church. The Presbyterian Church USA is a tradition proud of its concern for order. A classic situation relates to the number of governing boards that exist within a particular church organization. Many a newly ordained clergy-person has proceeded into the murky atmosphere of a particular board and has announced a rough plan to phase out this group. The effort is based on an identified conviction that a streamlined organizational structure is critical to navigate through the present-day disorder. An enormous amount of drag or friction is often encountered. The result of such a poorly designed effort, with little or no consideration of the environment, is the clergy-person fighting to maintain his or her future job status.

A key concept that assists in the identification of the resistance (or drag) that creates this form of friction is known as *pre-diagnostic analysis.* An understandable weakness of most professional schools is the failure to teach diagnostic skills. General principles and skills for specific vocations are transmitted, but the competencies necessary to introduce ideas into unique contexts are often neglected. Enthusiastic graduates take one-size-fits-all solutions, and attempt to force them into inappropriate environments. Through the educational process, passion is whipped up around some specific convictions, but inappropriate design and an incomplete reading of a specific context can sink many a new initiative before it leaves the harbor.

Pre-diagnostic analysis allows for the proper design of launched convictions. Whether in the home, workplace, community, or place of worship, those who really understand this concept will consider the big picture. They will shape initiatives based, not on a desire to manipulate or on ignorance, but on an accurate reading of the environment in which they must operate.

Update Your Friction Protection

The perspective of personal inertia that includes continual identification of friction is not a panacea for all pockets of ineffectiveness that infiltrate the various arenas of one's life. However, this perspective provides a description of an individual's life in harmony with the physical laws of the universe. Of course, these analogies are not intended to present a purely mechanical view of life, but rather an angle that brings synthesis and insight into how convictions of substance can maintain momentum.

Word of a computer virus potentially infecting hard drives brings waves of panic throughout a growing percentage of the developed world's population. For many, a PC seems to be virtually the only hope to manage the endless maze of continually proliferating data. The thought of not logging on and performing a number of electronic functions at nearly the speed of light can bring both child and adult to tears. An anti-virus program is mandatory to protect the operation of this lifeline.

The awareness of the basic forms of friction presented in this chapter: *sliding friction, rolling friction,* and *fluid friction,* and the forms through which they are expressed--*heat, noise, and structural breakdown*--increase our ability to maintain motion at optimal levels. Very few of us would think of submitting our computers to potential virus exposures without updated protection. It is even more important to take the same precautions for our identified convictions.

David and Kenneth Smazik

Habit: The Path of Least Resistance

In countless ways, we have learned through conditioning to seek the route of least resistance that creates the lowest levels of friction. These low-resistance trails become habits that form in our lives. We understand a habit to be a thought or behavior that has become as close as possible to involuntary—an action that takes place with little in the way of concentrated thought or effort to initiate. Whatever maintains motion through reduction of friction will occupy a prominent position and have a continual effect on a person's life. Such attitudes and behaviors can either induce a state of paralysis or maintain motion toward a life of impact.

Productive vs. Nonproductive Habits

Similar to the concept of inertia, a habit is a neutral reality. Just as the law of inertia refers both to the maintenance of inactivity and the maintenance of motion, habits may be thoughts and behaviors that are destructive and disruptive as well as thoughts and behaviors that are positive and productive. Pause for a few moments to inventory a few of the habits you exhibit each day.

One person's habit might consist of grabbing a six-pack of beer and a bag of chips after work and sitting all night on the couch watching TV while sipping and munching. Another person might have the habit of doing forty-five minutes of exercise after work, perusing a professional journal, and making a call or visit to a person who needs encouragement. Both sets of behaviors appear to have become automatic, but the long-term impact is considerably different.

One apparent difference that separates negative from positive habits relates to the origins of particular thoughts and behaviors. Many habitual negative thoughts and behaviors seem to develop out of no particularly premeditated reasoning process. Popular culture seems to support this trend with phrases such as, "Do what feels good" and "Whatever... ." Without a comprehensive sense of mission, and with a lack of discipline, now or for the future, gratification of short-term needs and desires becomes the motivating factor. In a sense, doing what feels good at the moment has become the conviction. There is low friction because nothing of substance has been placed in motion. Continual aimless wandering with no clear sense of purpose can become a habitual behavior, resulting in a form of paralysis.

Now for The Critical Connection

A positive habit appears to originate from intentional, premeditated thought. Identified convictions of substance develop because of the efforts committed to a dedicated inventory of our interior lives. A key element is the word *identified*. These convictions do not happen at the whim of passing immediate need, nor do they depend on which way the wind of current thought is blowing; they are clearly identified by the individual.

That which becomes habitual, whether based on ultimate purpose and impact or merely satiating immediate needs, has everything to do with reduction of friction. *A habit is essentially a thought or behavior that encounters little or no friction.* Anything that would impede or cause complete cessation of the habitual behavior has been minimized or removed. A particular atmosphere has been cleared of resistance to allow for maintenance of motion, momentum. Will that momentum be positive or negative? Productive or nonproductive?

Sliding into Habits

Let's see how the habit of consuming a six-pack of beer and a bag of chips each night flows freely from reductions in friction.

By design, the return route from work passes a discount liquor store and possibly a convenience store that often features a special deal on some form of snack. At home, no magazine, book, or TV program that deals with the destructive effects of high-calorie foods is available; although, an article extolling the positive benefits of moderate alcohol consumption may be tucked behind a magnet on the fridge. The bathroom scale was sold at a garage sale, and clothes that allow for ample room for expansion fill the closet.

Consider all the types of resistance that have been removed to reduce friction and readily allow this behavior to continue unimpeded, to gain the status of a habit. The challenge to locate beer and chips at a discount has been removed. Information that demonstrates a healthier way of life? Removed. A convenient way to measure extra pounds? Removed. The couch potato now experiences minimal friction from anger or frustration because the items are not readily available or are too costly. Guilt from the knowledge that another lifestyle, including moderate exercise and a better diet, would result in greater health is avoided. Resistance is minimized, friction reduced, and the way is opened for this destructive behavior to maintain motion. While some early signs of change are on the horizon, our commercial-saturated society currently appears to assist more readily in the minimization of resistance and reduction of friction that promotes habitual behaviors of this sort.

Momentum for Convictions

Let's use the same person referenced above in a second example. Positive convictions seem to take more concerted effort than negative ones, but they contain a larger purpose beyond immediate personal gratification. What will it take for such new convictions to obtain a level of momentum, to maintain speed and direction in a straight line, and to become a habitual part of this individual's life?

The newly identified conviction might consist of an awareness of those not able to help themselves within our society and a realization of the responsibility others should feel toward such individuals. In this particular case, let's say our friend recognizes the plight of elderly who have little or no social network because of the fragmentation of contemporary society.

Now that his new convictions have been identified, our former couch potato establishes a new route home from work. This one takes him past the home of a shut-in aunt. He now stops at least once a week for a visit. The passion around this conviction taps into a sense of purpose he has not previously known. The experience also brings him a broader life perspective and reduces the stress that builds during a day at work.

A local fruit and vegetable market is on the same street, so he combines a necessary shopping trip with his visits. He balances his caloric intake with proper nutrition and exercise. Pictures of his extended family members now have a place on his refrigerator. Not only does this weekly conversation have a very visible effect on the aunt, but also friends and family have been motivated to consider their own convictions. Momentum is clearly present.

Resistance has been reduced to allow for the free flow of a newly identified conviction. New behaviors have now become habitual. Proximity, convenience, a new sense of meaning in life—all contributed to a focus of energy or passion that encouraged the reduction of friction to allow for unimpeded motion of a conviction of substance.

Before we leave this section on ingrained habits consider a creative use of this perspective. While the primary focus has been on friction reduction to allow for the free flow of identified convictions, the creative use of resistance actually can prove beneficial in pursuit of a life of impact. Thoughts and behaviors that do not contribute to the motion of identified convictions can encounter numerous forms of *intentionally* constructed resistance.

Think again of the fictional individual used as a case study. An identified conviction of substance has replaced his somewhat mindless satisfaction of immediate personal desires. Additional resistance to his former lifestyle will inhibit it and keep the new way barrier free.

He can introduce photos and pieces of information to his living space that promote a healthy lifestyle. He may begin to participate in a weight-reduction program, including physical exercise that brings additional social pressure and resistance to bear against his former habits. A new wardrobe that represents a commitment of dollars will add further ammunition for him to resist sliding back into old patterns, and he may promise himself not to purchase any larger items if his new ones start to fit more tightly. He may then limit the amount of alcohol he consumes each week. If the new limit becomes difficult to maintain, he may add attendance at AA meetings to his schedule. When the motion of a life is understood from the perspective of resistance and friction, just as new ways are paved, destructive and disruptive patterns can be blocked.

This example in no way precludes the application of these concepts to other arenas. Home, family, vocation, religion, community—the reduction of resistance for unimpeded motion and the creative use of resistance to block unwanted behaviors applies to all. In all these arenas, thoughts and behaviors that represent identified convictions of substance can soon become automatic and habitual.

Questions

Chapter Eight

1. What comes to mind when you consider the concept of resistance and your inability to maintain motion toward effectiveness?

2. From the perspective of your world, identify the following forms of friction:
   - Sliding (Force applied in opposite direction):
   - Rolling (Greatly impedes motion):
   - Fluid (Creates drag):

3. What actions or thoughts encounter little or no friction within in your life? (Ingrained habits)

4. Think of creative and positive development of ingrained habits.

CHAPTER NINE

Arrival at Your Destination

"Talk is cheap."
"Are you just going to sit there?"

Consider a sports team that developed a well conceived game plan prior to their weekend contest. The plan was executed with a high level of energy and their successes continued to mount—momentum was clearly on their side. Does this team need to take a time-out to redesign their initial approach to the game and question their level of passion? They have proved to be successful. They now need to maintain their focus and energies on what is working, and on any possible scenarios that might slow their progress. What might possibly slow the momentum they have developed?

Efforts need to be concentrated on friction/resistance reduction. Rather than a continual clarification of identified convictions and the release of energy to place these convictions in motion, the central focus of effort becomes the reduction and removal of resistance.

Take a few minutes to review your life plan, the establishment of momentum in your life toward conviction-driven goals. The following summary will help identify sources of resistance, either in your environment or in your interior life.

Reduction of Friction—Chapter Eight

The most effective use of energy in the realm of reduction of resistance involves the prevention of friction. What confronts you head on and impairs your progress on your life's journey? What keeps you from the formation of habits that embody your convictions? Knowledge of the three common forms of friction is the place to start: sliding friction—a force applied in direct opposition to an object in motion; rolling friction—a force that impedes progress of a rolling object; and fluid friction—motion influenced by the amount of drag caused by numerous variables that include shape, material, speed, and viscosity.

The cause of resistance reduction will benefit greatly as individuals properly assess situations prior to the launch of a specific set of convictions. The intent of the basic conviction might be sound, but the form must be considered in light of a particular arena. In regard to the environment in which the conviction is launched, a lack of diagnostic work can result in people encountering numerous forms of resistance that could potentially be avoided. The current speed of societal change and the uniqueness of each context mandate this technique to avoid countless drags on our pursuit of purpose.

Signs of Wear and Tear—Chapter Seven

The sources of resistance delineated create the rub, or friction, against the motion of convictions. Friction converts the energy of motion into heat, noise, or material breakdown. Whether in the physical world or the metaphysical world, seek out heat, noise, or a materials/systems breakdown, and you will discover friction.

Consider the following manifestations of friction within the arenas of a person's life. In the heat of anger or rage, a sound and critical conviction encounters numerous forms of resistance. The result is complete cessation of motion. If additional acceleration is applied, the resistance also increases, and the point of contact creates high levels of emotional heat. The presence of these manifestations within the various arenas of a life is not difficult to identify, and this is a logical first place to begin in the reduction of resistance.

Noisy expressions of frustration and annoyance also signal the presence of friction. The friction can interfere with motion in a life as pervasively as the buildup of heat, or it may allow for minimal or constricted motion that in itself creates a high level of frustration. Again, the identification of frustration signals the presence of friction. To wallow in these frustrations consumes energy that could be better spent reducing the resistance that creates the environment for the presence of friction.

The breakdown of materials, a compromise of structural integrity, often signals a prolonged period of high-level friction. The breakdown of character is a radical expression of the presence of friction. Poor decision making, shortsighted solutions, and illegal activity—all often accompany this manifestation. Immediate intervention is necessary to identify the friction involved and to attend to the resistance present.

Restart When Stalled—Chapter Six

At whichever point of your life or in whichever previously mentioned realm, when motion ceases there are several potential obstacles to a restart. This cessation of motion often results from the buildup of friction due to the presence of resistance. The reasons for difficulty in getting started can involve inertia and other laws of the universe. In both its forms, inertia maintains whatever state is present. If an object is in motion, inertia tends to maintain its speed and direction in a straight line; but if an object is at rest, it will tend to maintain its inactivity. This is why a state of inactivity might appear natural and comfortable. There are other forces at work that can also make getting started difficult.

Gravity. Combined with the portion of the law of inertia that maintains inactivity, gravity creates a powerful force to hold us down. The current state of the world seems to strengthen the force of gravity.

Homeostasis. Another property that is inherent to individuals is the tendency of living things to create internal homeostasis. Systems work to create a state of balance to account for variations and to seek a place of stability or a comfort zone. Within a state of relative inactivity, in our analogy caused by gravity and maintained by inertia, a sense of comfort develops from the innate desire for balance. These forces account for the effort required to initiate motion and for the relative ease with which a state of inactivity is adopted when motion is impeded.

Follow the Direct Route—Chapter Five

The natural order of the universe can maintain the motion of an object in a straight line. The firing of a projectile illustrates this reality. A slight movement can push the object off course. What detours lure you off your path? To maximize this aspect of the created order, a personal mission statement is essential to maintain a straight line. Various course possibilities can reduce the efficiency of a conviction-driven focus and aid in the creation of resistance.

Avoid the Debris—Chapter Four

The debris that can litter the road you desire to travel are the fragmentation of systems and institutions, multiple options, data density, and the rapid pace of change. These factors can impede motion. These universal realities provide fertile soil for the sprouting of various forms of resistance, and they contribute to the downward gravitational pull exerted on life. When acknowledged and understood, the dynamics of inertia can maintain motion even through this contemporary maze.

Maintenance of Direction. With the current fragmentation of systems and institutions and the multiple options that vie for our attention, the ability to sustain direction and consistency becomes ever more important. The opportunity to experience motion through life by hitching a ride on a historic system or institution is no longer viable. Numerous worldwide tremors of all sorts have terminally cracked or crumbled most long-term structures, so there is not much left on which to grab. The recent explosion of options threatens continually to distract an individual from a specific destination. New developments cannot be ignored, but neither can the fact that the multitude of options can overwhelm and sink our identified convictions.

Maintenance of Speed. With the amount of data an individual must now filter, consistency of speed becomes an even greater challenge. The data-dense environment creates more information than the human brain can easily process. This tangle of data threatens to tie up all unsuspecting souls. While this component slows us down, the rate of speed at which all the above variables reproduce threatens to accelerate individuals to the point of burnout. Consciousness of pace is required so as not to allow contemporary life to spin convictions out of control.

Ready for Impact—Chapter Three

Amidst all the confusion that the current atmosphere throws at well-meaning individuals, a rather small group stands out: those who retain the secret to consistent effectiveness. These people live lives of impact while others suffer from paralysis of purpose. These individuals appear to possess an X-factor, an unknown quality that allows them to arrive with force even in the presence of countless forms of resistance.

In reality, this is not so much an X-factor but a *force* factor. The mass or substance of their convictions, multiplied by the passion with which these convictions are accelerated, results in a life of force. Force, or impact, increases and carries through even greater resistance: the greater the density of convictions times the rate of acceleration equals greater impact.

Build Your Speed—Chapter Two

The force of convictions is represented by a very simple equation. Concisely stated, if one does not possess passion, the energy to accelerate convictions, there is no fuel to create the force that results in impact. While convictions cannot always push through the entire complement of encountered resistance, high velocity arising from a passion to reach the goal often propels those convictions through barriers that stall a great majority of people.

A person with a passion can think of nothing else. A case of myopic vision develops—all else fades from view, and the object of passion stands alone in the field of vision. With this viewpoint comes a longing to remain in the presence of the desired object; one is said to have a singular focus. This fixation leads to the willingness to sacrifice all else for the object of desire (or the objective). There are no lengths to which the person with passion will not go to achieve this object or outcome.

Throughout history, great lives of impact have had in common the presence of passion. The combination of elements that constituted this passion may engender various descriptions, yet some form of myopic vision, obsession, and sacrifice existed.

Prepare For the Journey—Chapter One

Without an identified destination, life becomes nothing more than endless wandering. A life of impact begins with a clear destination, with identified convictions—not convictions that represent a haphazard collection of interests, but convictions that contain a high level of density.

This is where it all begins, the start of the journey. If convictions of substance are identified and accelerated with passion, a life will arrive at its goals with force of impact. Not all resistance along the way will fade, but a developed *will* can break through many forms of resistance that threaten to impede motion.

To develop the density of one's convictions requires intentional work—evaluation of core beliefs and values distilled through emotional and spiritual maturity. Without this interior inventory, convictions run the risk of becoming no more than hot air. Recall the cannonball from earlier chapters. Convictions that represent density of principle and purpose stand the best chance of powering through the walls of resistance.

Build Your Momentum!

In response to those who believe that everything happens by chance and not under the influence of specific laws of nature, Albert Einstein made the following comment: "You believe in God playing dice, and I in the perfect laws in the

David and Kenneth Smazik

world of things existing as real objects, which I try to grasp in a wildly speculative way."[30]

May our journeys reach their destinations by the increase in the force of our convictions, consistently and efficiently, and through the vigilance of continual identification of friction from the perspective of least-resistance planning. This set of skills requires energy (a limited resource) to allow the laws of inertia to maintain motion, to build momentum for your identified convictions. Refinement of convictions and the force of passion to break the gravitational pull remain constants in this process, but they should not become the sole focus of our efforts. The identification and reduction of resistance allows our convictions to arrive at their destinations with maximum impact.

"Where there is a will, there is a way."

"This time will be different!"

Questions

Chapter Nine

1. Was there a time in your life when the "game plan" appeared to be effective?

2. Assuming that your convictions are sound (dense) and are accelerated by sufficient passion, which identified resistance will you need to reduce?

3. Build your Life Momentum using the concepts presented in each chapter:

Part One—Discover the Essentials to Get Going

      Ch. 1 – Identify your convictions.
      Ch. 2 – Where does your passion lie?
      Ch. 3 – Create a picture of impact in your life.

Part Two—Discover What Keeps You Going

      Ch. 4 – How can you maintain consistent direction and speed?
      Ch. 5 – How can you maintain straight-line efficiency in your life?
      Ch. 6 – Spot the places where you remain stuck in neutral.

Part Three—Discover What Slows You Down

      Ch. 7 – Identify the heat, noise and breakdown of integrity in your life.
      Ch. 8 –What opposes your momentum toward a life of impact?
      Ch. 9 – With resistances reduced, where does your life arrive?

REFERENCES

[1] N.E. Thing Enterprises (1995). *Magic Eye Gallery, A Showing of 88 Images.* Kansas City, KS: Andrews and McMeel

[2] Delbecq. A. L. (2002). "Comments on Karen Ayas, Creating High-Performing Organizations: A Conversation with Roger Saillant", *Reflections. 3 (2),* (pp.12-13).

[3] McGraw, P. C. (2001). *Self Matters: Creating Your Life from the Inside Out.* (pp. 252-253) NY: Free Press.

[4] Thurman, C. (1999). *The Lies We Believe.* (p. 23) Nashville, TN: Thomas Nelson.

[5] Corey, G. (1986). *Theory and Practice of Counseling and Psycho-therapy, (3rd ed.).* (pp. 212-213) Monterey, CA: Brooke/Cole

[6] Bly, R. (1996). *The Sibling Society.* NY: Random House

[7] Goleman, D. (1997). *Emotional Intelligence.* NY: Bantam Book.

[8] Hawking, S. W. (1988). *A Brief History of Time: From the Big Bang to Black Holes.* (p. 108) NY: Bantam

[9] Gladwell, M. (2000). *The Tipping Point: How Little Things Can Make A Big Difference.* Little, Brown

[10] Putman, R. D. (2000). *Bowling Alone: The Collapse and Revival of American Community.* (p. 216) NY: Simon & Schuster

[11] Churchill, W. (1940). *First Speech As Prime Minister, May 13, 1940 to House of Commons.* Retrieved March 3, 2005 from http://www.winstonchurchill.org/i4a/pages/index.cfm?pageid=391

[12] Churchill, W. (1940). *First Speech As Prime Minister, May 13, 1940 to House of Commons.* Retrieved March 3, 2005 from http://www.winstonchurchill.org/i4a/pages/index.cfm?pageid=391

[13] Edelman, M. W. (2002). Corkin Cherubini in C. Kennedy (ed.) *Profiles In Courage for Our Time.* (p. 154) NY: Hyperion.

[14] Mother Teresa of Calcutta (n.d.). Retrieved March 3, 2005 from http://feastofsaints.com/whypray.htm

[15] Mother Teresa of Calcutta (n.d.). Retrieved July 6, 2005 from http://magnificat.ca/english/mteresa.htm

[16] Collins, J. (2001). *Good To Great.* (pp. 19-20) NY: HarperCollins.

[17] Goleman, D., McKee, A., and Boyatzis, R. E. (2002). *Primal Leadership: Realizing the Power of Emotional Intelligence.* (p. 57) Boston, MA: Harvard Business School Publishing.

[18] Alcoholics Anonymous World Services, Inc. (2005). *The Twelve Steps of Alcoholics Anonymous.* NY: Author. Retrieved July 6, 2005 from http://www.aa.org/default/en_about_aa_sub.cfm?subpageid=84&pageid=13

[19] Prochaska, J. O., Norcorss, J. C., and DiClemente, C. O. (1994). *Changing For Good.* NY: Avon.

[20] Covey, S. R. (1989). *The Seven Habits of Highly Effective People: Restoring the Character Ethic.* NY: Simon and Schuster.

[21] Collins, J. (2001). *Good To Great.* (p. 39) NY: HarperCollins.

[22] Collins, J. (2001). *Good To Great.* (p. 39) NY: HarperCollins.

[23] Blanchard, K. (1981). *The One Minute Manager.* NY: William Morrow.

[24] Lovell, J., & Jeffrey, K. (1994). *Lost Moon: The Perilous Voyage of Apollo 13.* Boston, MA: Houghton Mifflin.

[25] Strauss, W., & Howe, N. (1991). *Generations: The History of America's Future, 1584 to 2069.* NY: William Morrow.

[26] Jones, D. (1999). *Everyday Creativity* [Training Video]. (Available from http://www.dewittjones.com/html/training.shtml)

[27] Willard, D. (1988). *The Spirit of the Disciplines: Understanding How God Changes Lives.* NY: HarperCollins

[28] Trompenaars, F., & Hampden-Turner, C. (2002). *21 leaders from the 21st Century: How Innovative Leaders Manage in the Digital Age.* (p. 147). NY: McGraw Hill

[29] Cherniss, C., & Adler, M. (2000). *Promoting Emotional Intelligence in Organizations: Make Training in Emotional Intelligence Effective.* (p. 19) Alexandria, VA: ASTD

[30] Schlipp, P. (1969). *Albert Einstein, Philosopher-Scientist.* (p. 176) London: Cambridge University Press.

ABOUT THE AUTHOR

Life Momentum is a synthesis of common elements, encompassed and defined by a truth of the universe, that stretch across vocational disciplines. The authors' careers are a result of the creation of momentum in two diverse work environments. Kenneth, who holds an engineering degree and an MBA will shortly earn a master's degree in psychology, and is credited with various patents. His current position with a major corporation involves a working relationship with a large customer. David possesses master's degrees in divinity and counseling psychology and a doctorate in ministry. He is presently co-pastor of a mainline church that has sustained forward motion in an era in which a majority of similar churches struggle to maintain survival.

You can contact the authors at lifemomentum.org.

Printed in the United States
52937LVS00003B/182

9 781420 876161